D1259763

UNCOLLECTED WRITINGS

KENNIKAT PRESS SCHOLARLY REPRINTS

Dr. Ralph Adams Brown, Senior Editor

Series on

LITERARY AMERICA IN THE NINETEENTH CENTURY

Under the General Editorial Supervision of
Dr. Walter Harding
University Professor, State University of New York

The Emerson Library in Concord.

UNCOLLECTED WRITINGS

ESSAYS, ADDRESSES, POEMS, REVIEWS AND LETTERS

BY

RALPH WALDO EMERSON

KENNIKAT PRESS
Port Washington, N. Y./London

UNCOLLECTED WRITINGS

First published in 1912
Reissued in 1971 by Kennikat Press
Library of Congress Catalog Card No: 71-122652
ISBN 0-8046-1300-1

Manufactured by Taylor Publishing Company Dallas, Texas

INTRODUCTION

For many years the editor, in common with other collectors of American first editions, has known of the existence of much Emerson material that has never been permanently placed in book form or gathered in any collected edition of Emerson's Works. As early as 1866 an edition of Emerson appeared in London labelled "Complete Works," but, though much matter was crowded into the two volumes, it was very incomplete. In 1869, 1876, 1881 and 1883 collected editions appeared, bearing the imprints of Fields, Osgood & Company and their various successors, but on these editions no claims were made as to completeness. In 1884 Houghton, Mifflin & Co., of Boston, published a twelve-volume edition of Emerson called the Riverside Edition, labelling it "The Complete Works." This edition was edited by J. E. Cabot, but while Mr. Cabot included in the Riverside Edition much material that had never before been published in book form, he failed to include a great mass of material, essays, addresses, speeches and poems, which he must have known existed.

In 1903-4 Houghton, Mifflin & Co. issued the Centenary Edition of Emerson, in twelve volumes, the work being edited by Edward Waldo Emerson. This edition contains much matter not included in the previous Riverside Edition, but, although the publishers again claimed completeness for their book, they again neglected to include all known material.

As the matter stands to-day, no such thing as a really complete edition of Emerson has ever been issued, no matter what publishers' title-pages may say or claim.

This present volume contains nothing but authentic Emerson material not appearing in any of the collected editions or in any of the so-called "Complete Works." Many of the pieces in this volume are of great importance and should have been given to the public long ago. The initial piece, "Nature," is an individual essay, distinct from all others of the same or similar title, and appeared in "The Boston Book" in 1850. The article on Amos Bronson Alcott was written for the "New American Cyclopedia" in 1858. Emerson's address entitled "The Right Hand of Fellowship," and his addresses at the Japanese Banquet, the Froude Dinner and the Bryant Festival, are all important and worthy of preservation. Previous editors have reprinted Emerson on Carlyle's "Past and Present," but have overlooked his Review of Carlyle's "French Revolution."

During the years 1840 to 1844 Emerson contributed liberally to "The Dial," a quarterly magazine published in Boston. More than seventy-five pieces of Emerson's writings, including essays, poems and reviews, appeared in this magazine during the four years of its existence, and this material has been largely drawn upon, but not exhausted by the various Emerson editors. In this present volume we have reprinted from "The Dial" all of the papers omitted by previous editors, and they are thirty-two in number.

Included in this volume are six poems that have not been reprinted since their first appearance in the early annuals where they were first published. A number of Emerson's letters conclude this volume, two of them being of special importance. One is the Letter to the Second Church and Society, March,

1829, accepting the invitation to become pastor of that church, and the other is the Letter to the Second Church and Society, dated December, 1832, addressed to the congregation after he had delivered his famous sermon entitled " The Lord's Supper," on September 9th, 1832, which was followed by his resignation.

CONTENTS

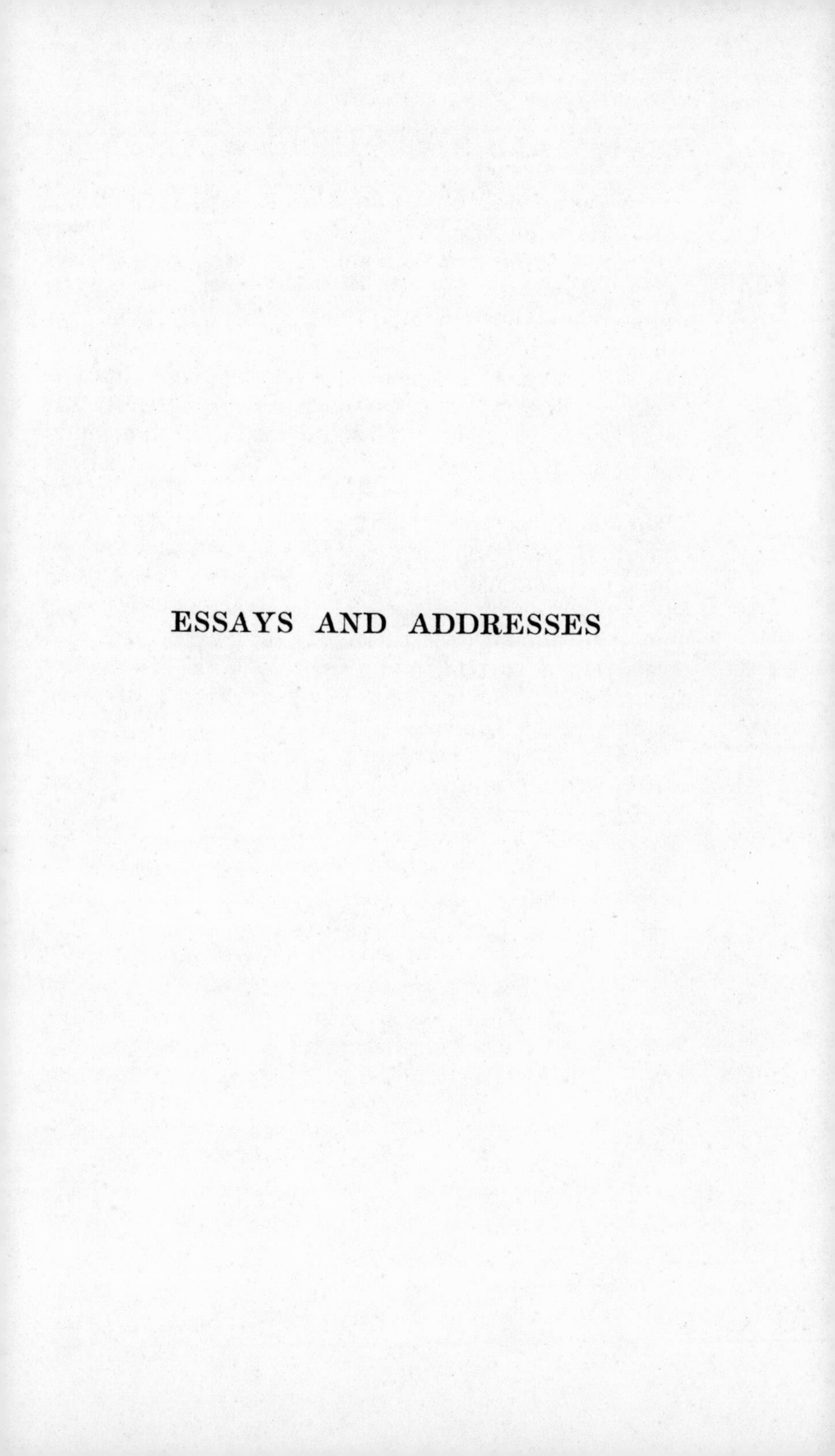

ESSAYS AND ADDRESSES

NATURE

There are days which occur in this climate, at almost any season of the year, wherein the world reaches its perfection, when the air, the heavenly bodies, and the earth, make a harmony, as if nature would indulge her offspring; when, in these bleak upper sides of the planet, nothing is to desire that we have heard of the happiest latitudes, and we bask in the shining hours of Florida and Cuba; when everything that has life gives signs of satisfaction, and the cattle that lie on the ground seem to have great and tranquil thoughts. These halcyons may be looked for with a little more assurance in that pure October weather, which we distinguish by the name of the Indian Summer. The day, immeasurably long, sleeps over the broad hills and warm wide fields. To have lived through all its sunny hours, seems longevity enough. The solitary places do not seem quite lonely. At the gates of the forest, the surprised man of the world is forced to leave his city estimates of great and small, wise and foolish. The knapsack of custom falls off his back with the first step he makes into these precincts. Here is sanctity which shames our religions, and reality which discredits our heroes. Here we find nature to be the circumstance which dwarfs every other circumstance, and judges like a god all men that come to her. We have crept out of our close and crowded houses into the night and morning, and we see what majestic beauties daily wrap us in their bosom. How willingly we would escape the barriers which render them comparatively impotent, escape the sophistication and second thought, and suffer nature to entrance us. The tempered light of the woods is like a perpetual morning, and is stimulating and heroic. The anciently reported spells of these places creep on us. The stems of pines, hemlocks, and oaks, almost gleam like iron on the excited eye. The incommunicable trees begin to persuade us to live with them, and quit our life of solemn trifles. Here no history, or church, or state, is interpolated on the divine sky and the immortal year. How easily we might walk onward into the opening landscape, absorbed by new pictures, and by thoughts fast succeeding each other, until by degrees the recollection of home was crowded out of the mind, all memory obliterated by the tyranny of the present, and we were led in triumph by nature.

These enchantments are medicinal, they sober and heal us. These are plain pleasures, kindly and native to us. We come to our own, and make friends with matter, which the ambitious chatter of the schools would persuade us to despise. We never can part with it; the mind loves its old home; as water to our thirst, so is the rock, the ground, to our eyes, and hands, and feet. It is firm water; it is cold flame: what health, what affinity! Ever an old friend, ever like a dear friend and brother, when we chat affectedly with strangers, comes in this honest face, and takes a grave liberty with us, and shames us out of our nonsense. Cities give not the human senses room enough. We go out daily and nightly to feed the eyes on the horizon, and require so much scope, just as we need water for our bath. There are all degrees of natural influence, from these quarantine powers of nature, up to her dearest and gravest ministrations to the imagination and the soul. There is the bucket of cold water from the spring, the wood-fire to which the chilled traveller rushes for safety, — and there is the sublime moral of autumn and of noon. We nestle in nature, and draw our living as parasites from her roots and grains, and we receive glances from the heavenly bodies, which call us to solitude, and foretell the remotest future. The blue zenith is the point in which romance and reality meet. I think, if we should be rapt away into all that we dream of heaven, and should converse with Gabriel and Uriel, the upper sky would be all that would remain of our furniture.

It seems as if the day was not wholly profane, in which we have given heed to some natural object. The fall of snowflakes in a still air, preserving to each crystal its perfect form; the blowing of sleet over a wide sheet of water, and over plains, the waving rye-field, the mimic waving of acres of houstonia, whose innumerable florets whiten and ripple before the eye; the reflections of trees and flowers in glassy lakes; the musical steaming odorous south wind, which converts all trees to wind-harps; the crackling and spurting of hemlock in the flames; or of pine logs, which yield glory to the walls and faces in the sitting-room, — these are the music and pictures of the most ancient religion. My house stands in low land, with limited outlook, and on the skirt of the village. But I go with my friend to the shore of our little river, and with one stroke of the paddle, I leave the village politics and personalities behind, and pass into a delicate realm of sunset and moonlight, too bright almost for spotted man to enter without novitiate and probation. We penetrate bodily this incredible beauty: we dip our hands in this painted element: our eyes are bathed in these lights and forms. A holiday, a villeggiatura, a royal revel, the proudest, most heart-rejoicing festival that valor and beauty, power and taste, ever decked and enjoyed, establishes itself on the instant. These sunset clouds, these delicately emerging stars, with their private and ineffable glances, signify it and proffer it. I am taught the poorness of our invention, the ugliness of towns and palaces. Art and luxury have early learned that they must work as enhancement and sequel to this original beauty. I am over instructed for my return. Henceforth I shall be hard to please. I cannot go back to toys. I am grown expensive and sophisticated. I can no longer live without elegance: but a countryman shall be my master of revels. He who knows the most, he who knows what sweets and virtues are in the ground, the waters, the plants, the heavens, and how to come at these enchantments, is the rich and royal man. Only as far as the masters of the world have called in nature to their aid, can they reach the height of magnificence. This is the meaning of their hanging-gardens, villas, garden-houses, islands, parks, and preserves, to back their faulty personality with these strong accessories. I do not wonder that the landed interest should be invincible in the state with these dangerous auxiliaries. These bribe and invite; not kings, not palaces, not men, not women, but these tender and poetic stars, eloquent of secret promises. We heard what the rich man said, we knew of his villa, his grove, his wine, and his company, but the provocation and point of the invitation came out of these beguiling stars. In their soft glances, I see what men strove to realize in some Versailles, or Paphos, or Ctesiphon. Indeed, it is the magical lights of the horizon, and the blue sky for the background, which save all our works of art, which were otherwise baubles. When the rich tax the poor with servility and obsequiousness, they should consider the effect of men, reputed to be the possessors of nature, on imaginative minds. Ah! if the rich were rich as the poor fancy riches! A boy hears a military band play on the field at night, and he has kings and queens, and famous chivalry palpably before him. He hears the echoes of a horn in a hill country, in the Notch Mountains, for example, which converts the mountains into an Æolian harp, and this supernatural *tiralira* restores to him the Dorian mythology, Apollo, Diana, and all divine hunters and huntresses. Can a musical note be so lofty, so haughtily beautiful? To the poor young poet, thus fabulous is his picture of society; he is loyal; he respects the rich; they are rich for the sake of his imagination; how poor his fancy would be, if they were not rich! That they have some high-fenced grove, which they call a park; that they live in larger and better garnished saloons than he has visited, and go in coaches, keeping only the society of the elegant, to watering-places, and to distant cities, are the groundwork from which he has delineated estates of romance, compared with which their actual possessions are shanties and paddocks. The muse herself betrays her son, and enhances the gifts of wealth and well born beauty, by a radiation out of the air, and clouds, and forests that skirt the road, — a certain haughty favor, as if from patrician genii to patricians, a kind of aristocracy in nature, a prince of the power of the air.

The moral sensibility which makes Edens and Tempes so easily, may not be always found, but the material landscape is never far off. We can find these enchantments without visiting the Como Lake, or the Madeira Islands. We exaggerate the praises of local scenery. In every landscape, the point of astonishment is the meeting of the sky and the earth, and that is seen from the first hillock as well as from the top of the Alleghanies. The stars at night stoop down over the brownest, homliest common, with all the spiritual magnificence which they shed on the Campagna, or on the marble deserts of Egypt. The uprolled clouds and the colors of morning and evening, will transfigure maples and alders. The difference between landscape and landscape is small, but there is great difference in the beholders. There is nothing so wonderful in any particular landscape, as the necessity of being beautiful under which every landscape lies. Nature cannot be surprised in undress. Beauty breaks in everywhere.

AMOS BRONSON ALCOTT

Amos Bronson Alcott, a philosopher devoted to the science of education, was born at Wolcott, Conn., Nov. 29, 1799. Like many farmers' sons in Connecticut, whilst still a boy, he was intrusted by a local trader with a trunk of merchandise, with which he sailed for Norfolk, Va., and which he afterward carried about among the plantations; and his early readings were in the planters' houses, who gave hospitality to the young salesman, and, observing his turn for study, talked with him, and opened their bookcases to him in a stormy day. On his return to Connecticut he began to teach, and attracted attention by his success with an infant-school.

He removed to Boston in 1828, and showed singular skill and sympathy in his methods of teaching young children of five, six and seven years of age, at the Masonic Temple. (See a printed account, "Record of a School," E. P. Peabody, 12mo, Boston, 1834; also, a transcript of the colloquies of these children with their teacher, in "Conversations on the Gospels," 2 volumes, 12mo, Boston, 1836.) But the school was in advance of public opinion, and, on the publication of this book, was denounced by the newspapers of the day. After closing his school, Mr. Alcott removed to Concord, Mass., where he betook himself to his studies, interesting himself chiefly in natural theology, and the various questions of reform, in education, in diet, civil and social institutions.

On the invitation of James P. Greaves, of London, the friend and fellow-laborer of Pestalozzi in Switzerland, Mr. Alcott went to England in 1842. Mr. Greaves died before his arrival, but Mr. Alcott was cordially received by his friends who had given his name to their school at "Alcott House," Ham, near London, and spent some months in making acquaintance with various classes of reformers. On his return to America, he brought with him two of his English friends, Charles Lane and H. G. Wright; and Mr. Lane having bought a farm which he called "Fruitlands," at Harvard, Mass., they all went there to found a new community. Messrs. Lane and Wright soon returned to England, and the farm was sold. Mr. Alcott removed to Boston, and has led the life of a Peripatetic philosopher, conversing in cities and in villages, wherever invited, on divinity, on human nature, on ethics, on dietetics, and a wide range of practical questions. These conversations, which were at first casual, gradually assumed a more formal character, the topics being often printed on cards, and the company meeting at a fixed time and place.

Mr. Alcott attaches great importance to diet and government of the body; still more to race and complexion. He is an idealist, and we should say Platonist, if it were not doing injustice to give any name implying secondariness to the highly original habit of his salient and intuitive mind. He has singular gifts for awakening contemplation and aspiration in simple and in cultivated persons. Though not learned, he is a rare master of the English language; and, though no technical logician, he has a subtle and deep science of that which actually passes in thought, and thought is ever seen by him in its relations to life and morals. Those persons who are best prepared by their own habit of thought, set the highest value on his subtle perception and facile generalization.

RIGHT HAND OF FELLOWSHIP

AT ORDINATION OF HERSEY BRADFORD GOODWIN, 1830

THE ancient custom of offering a new pastor the expression of the sympathy of the churches is no unsuitable rite in the ceremonies of ordination, and hath a deep foundation in reason. There is no sympathy so strong as that which exists between the good, and this fellow-feeling Christianity has done all to foster. Whilst men are in the moral darkness which vice produces, each individual is a sect by himself; each is a self-seeker, with his hands against every man, and every man's hands against him. Each, forgetful of all other rights and feelings, is straining every nerve to build up his own sordid advantage, and tearing down his neighbor's happiness, if need be, to build up his own. His eye is blind, his ear is deaf to the great harmonies by which God yoked together the social and the selfish good of his children.

Just in proportion as men grow wiser and better, their efforts converge to a point. For as truth is one, in seeking it, they all aim to conform their action to one standard. When intelligent men talk together, it is remarkable how much they think alike, how many propositions are taken for granted, that are disputed, word by word, in the conversation of ignorant persons. The more enlightened men are, the greater is this unanimity, as is attested by the common wonder when two minds of unquestionable elevation come to opposite conclusions. As it is with the mind, so is it with the heart. As two minds agreeing with truth do mutually agree, so, if their affections are right with God, they will be true to one another.

Christianity aims to teach the perfection of human nature, and eminently therefore does it teach the unity of the spirit. It is, not only in its special precepts, but by all its operations, a law of love. It does, by its revelation of God and of the true purposes and the true rules of life, operate to bind up, to join together, and not to distinguish and separate. It proclaimed peace. But it speaks first to its own disciples, "Be of one mind," else with what countenance should the church say to the world of men, Love one another. And thousands and thousands of hearts have heard the commandment, and anon with joy received it. All men on whose souls the light of God's revelation truly shineth, with whatever apparent differences, are substantially of one mind, work together, whether consciously or not, for one and the same good. Faces that never beheld each other are lighted by it with the same expression. Hands that were never clasped toil unceasingly at the same work. This it is which makes the omnipotence of truth in the keeping of feeble men, — this fellowship in all its servants, this swift, consenting acknowledgment with which they hail it when it appears. God's truth, — it is that electric spark which flies instantaneously through the countless hands that compose the chain. Truth — not like each form of error, depending for its repute on the powers and influence of here and there a solitary mind that espouses it — combines hosts for its support, and makes them co-operate across mountains and oceans, — yea, and ages of time. This is what was meant in that beautiful sentiment of ancient philosophy, that God had so intimately linked all wise men to each other that, if one should only lift his finger in Rome, all the rest were benefited by it, through Egypt or Asia. This is what was meant by that *one body in Christ,* of which all his disciples are *the members.* Sir, it is this sentiment which is recognized in the ancient and simple rite of the churches.

God has bound heart to heart by invisible and eternal bands, by oneness of nature, of duty, and of hope. To us is "One Lord, one faith, one baptism." And, in acknowledgment of these divine connections existing between us, the Christian churches, whose organ I am, do offer you, my brother, this right hand of their fellowship. They greet you, by me, to the exalted relations on which now you are entering. They give you a solemn welcome to great duties, to honorable sacrifices, to unremitting studies, and to the eternal hope of all souls. They exhort you to all pious resolutions; and they pledge to you, by this sign, their sympathy, their aid, and their intercession.

They say to you that, so long as in purity of heart you do the work of God in this vineyard of his, you are not alone; but you shall be secure of the love and the furtherance, not of these churches only, but of all righteous men. In every hour of perplexity or affliction, they shall encourage and aid and bless you, by desire and by word and by action. And when the day of success comes to you, and you see around you in this garden of the Lord, the fruit of your virtues and the light of your example and the truth you teach shine forth together, in that day a kindred joy shall touch our hearts, — we shall be glad with you, and give thanks with you, and hope for you.

Sir, it is with sincere pleasure that I speak for the churches on this occasion and on this spot, hallowed to all by so many patriotic and to me by so many affectionate recollections. I feel a peculiar, a personal right to welcome you hither to the home and the temple of my fathers. I believe the church whose pastor you are will forgive me the allusion, if I express the extreme interest which every man feels in the scene of the trials and labors of his ancestors. Five out of seven of your predecessors are my kindred. They are in the dust who bind my attachment to this place, but not all. I cannot help congratulating you that one survives, to be to you the true friend and venerable counsellor he has ever been to me.

I heartily rejoice to see their labors and a portion of his resting on one who comes with such ability, and, as I trust, with such devout feeling to the work. Suffer me then, *as for them,* to offer you my hand, and receive with it, my brother, my best wishes and prayers for your success in your great undertaking and for your everlasting welfare.

ADDRESS AT JAPANESE BANQUET, AUG. 2, 1872

MR. PRESIDENT AND GENTLEMEN: — I feel honored by serving as the mouth-piece of this company for a moment. The great deserts of this occasion and the interest of this company might inspire a greater coward than myself.

I shall share with this company the respect with which they regard this embassy. It is full of romance to us. Hitherward come a people with whom our history has been but little occupied, a people who have hidden themselves in their slow and private national growth. It is six hundred years, as I understand, since Marco Polo saw on the shores of the Yellow Sea one great island, and that island was one of the three islands of Japan — Niphon and Yesso and Kiovsoa. Columbus, it seems, took this book of Marco Polo in his hands, and when he arrived at Cuba he thought he had arrived at Japan. He had not come there, but he showed mankind the way from thence to Japan, and President Fillmore found it. Not, I think, until 1852 was Commodore Perry sent by President Fillmore to make a treaty with Japan, so slow was the progress of our acquaintance with the nation whose representatives we greet to-night.

There is something very interesting in the history of that nation. I remember that in my college days our professor in Greek used to tell us always in his record of history, "All tends to the mysterious East;" and so slow was the progress that only now are the threads gathered up of relation between the farthest East and the farthest West. The nation has itself every claim on us. The singular selection that it showed in appealing to America for its guidance and assistance in western civilization, the brave and simple manner in which it has sent its pupils, its young men, to our schools and colleges and to learn our arts, is a great honor to their wisdom and their noble heart. There is humanity as well as there is ambition. I am very glad to be apprised by very competent critics in art that in certain arts there has been no such success in other nations as in Japan, that their bronzes, and not only so but the arts of design when applied to outline drawings, are more masterly than are to be found in Europe or America. And I have to say that I think the American government and American history owes great thanks to the enlightened policy of President Fillmore who, in 1852, sent Commodore Perry to that country and introduced a new thought into his embassy. Instead of sending to what he supposed a comparatively foreign and unrelated country, to say the least, to the civil nations — instead of sending to them beads and rum barrels, he sent the best of our civilization. He sent the very best instruments and inventions that the country could command. He sent the steamboat. He sent the telescope. He sent the telegraph. He sent all those instruments and machines which had lately attracted and strengthened western civilization. This gift was gratefully and nobly received, instantly understood and remade in that country. There is something besides art in Japan that is interesting — namely, a certain strength in the constitution and the character of the Japanese, which seems to have been revealed by many of these emigrant scholars who have honored our country; namely, a certain force of mind allied to religion which marks their fidelity to their chiefs. I understand that if a young man in Japan finds that he cannot raise the young man whom he has undertaken to guard and attend to an equality to the very best of his class, and if he cannot raise him above those who are not his equal in rank, he suffers so much pain that he cannot return to that country; and he is drawn into a resolution that is self-sacrifice, and is prepared for the suicide of himself rather than that his fidelity to his chieftain should fail. It is a very remarkable trait. We don't understand it in our loose, mercantile, popular civilization, but it is a prodigious power to those people that possess it. One thing was said to me in relation to this very interesting company of our friends — this: That they are, more than others, deeply interested in education. They have, indeed, honored me — I am quite undeserving of that honor — with enquiries in regard to that I wish I could help them. I wish any of us could. The best advice I can give to them is to say that next week, in this city, I understand, is to be held a meeting of the National Board of Education, in which, among other gentlemen and officers, is Mr. Harris of St. Louis in Missouri, who is the head there of the city education and is besides the editor of the only journal of speculative philosophy edited in this country; a very learned and a very able man, and very able as I understand in this particular subject of education.

I should wish my friends to make his acquaintance, as I doubt not he would be very glad to make theirs. I don't know any person that could advise them better on the subject.

Note — This address was given at the banquet given at the Revere House, Boston, on August 2, 1872.

ADDRESS AT THE JAMES ANTHONY FROUDE DINNER

AT DELMONICO'S, NEW YORK, OCTOBER 15, 1872

I CONFESS, Mr. Chairman and gentlemen, that I have accepted your invitation to this banquet in good faith and humble belief that my friend, Mr. Froude, of old times, was coming here, but not to be myself made in any manner the subject of extravagant eulogy, in the poetic or satirical spirit of the President. To that I have nothing to reply, excepting that I know nothing of it. It gives me great pleasure, certainly, to be present at this very highly proper reception of our guest. I had the great pleasure many, many years ago — it was twenty-four years ago — of meeting him when he was new from his Exeter college, and amid very valued friends, Mr. Clough of Oriel, honored in all parts of this country where intelligent young scholars are known; Mr. Arnold of this same college, also of Oriel, whose fame is also in all our mouths; Mr. Stanley of Exeter; Mr. Palgrave, and other able young men with whom I became most happily acquainted on my visit at Oxford. And I rejoice very much to see Mr. Froude's face here, with all our added acquaintance with him in his books. His history is well-known, I know, to all good readers in this country, and he has established the importance of his own opinion, of his own judgment, in these books. I think he has taught us much. He has shown at least two eminent faculties in his histories — the faculty of seeing wholes, and the faculty of seeing and saying particulars. The one makes history valuable, and the other makes it readable — interesting. Both these qualities his writings have eminently shown. I think we are indebted to him for a power which is eminent in them, the discretion which is given us — the speeches, the language of the very persons whom his history records. The language, the style of the books, draws very much of its excellence from that habit, that practice, of giving the very language of the times. He knows well that the old English people and Irish people of whom his history records the events, did not write or speak in the style of *The Edinburgh Review* or *The North American Review,* but that they spoke a stern and dreadful language, when words were few and when words meant much. So that the language is like the cry of the soldier when the battle begins, or the cry of the fugitive when the battle turns against him. It is a pithy and wonderful language. If you remember, it is Shakespeare that says: "When breath is scant, it's very seldom spent in vain." That is the very language of the poet. And that is the language which his taste and judgment has had the skill to secure, giving an emphasis and power to his history, which is not familiar to English and Irish history.

It gives me great pleasure to see Mr. Froude, an old friend, because he recalls the time of my own visit, twenty-four years ago. It was at Oxford, when I knew his contemporaries, his fellow-students at Exeter and Oriel — Mr. Arnold, Mr. Stanley, Mr. Clough — alas, he died too early for us all — Mr. Palgrave, and many other young men, then of great promise, and some of them who have more than fulfilled that promise. It gives me great pleasure to remember that time, and to see that, if something has fallen, much has survived, and that we have here one of the best representatives of just that culture and just that power and moral determination which was exhibited and felt by all those young men.

SPEECH AT THE BRYANT FESTIVAL AT "THE CENTURY," NOVEMBER 5, 1864

Mr. President: — Whilst I am grateful to you and to "The Century" for the privilege of joining you in this graceful and most deserved homage to our poet, I am a little disconcerted, in the absence of some expected friends from the Bay State, at finding myself put forward to speak on their part. Let me say for them that we have a property in his genius and virtue. Whilst we delight in your love of him, and in his power and reputation in your imperial State, we can never forget that he was born on the soil of Massachusetts. Your great metropolis is always, by some immense attraction of gravity, drawing to itself our best men. But we forgive you in this case the robbery, when we see how nobly you have used him. Moreover, the joint possession by New York and Massachusetts of him, and of others in this great circle of his friends, is one of those ethereal hoops which bind these states inseparably in these perilous times.

I join with all my heart in your wish to honor this native, sincere, original, patriotic poet. I say original: I heard him charged with being of a certain school. I heard it with surprise, and asked, what school? for he reminded me of Goldsmith, or Wordsworth, or Byron, or Moore. I found him always original, a true painter of the face of this country, and of the sentiment of his own people. When I read the verses of popular American and English poets, I often think that they appear to have gone into the Art Galleries and to have seen pictures of mountains, but this man to have seen mountains.

With his stout staff he has climbed Greylock and the White Hills, and sung what he saw. He renders Berkshire to me in verse, with the sober coloring, too, to which nature cleaves, only now and then permitting herself the scarlet and gold of the prism. It is his proper praise, that he first and he only made known to mankind our northern landscape — its summer splendor, its autumn russet, its winter lights and glooms. And he is original because he is sincere. Many young men write verse which strikes by talent, but the writer has not committed himself, the man is not there, it is written at arm's length, he could as well have written on any other theme: it was not necessitated and autobiographic, and therefore it does not imprint itself on the memory, and return for thought and consolation in our solitary hours. But our friend's inspiration is from the inmost mind; he has not a labial but a chest voice, and you shall detect the tastes and experiences of the poem in his daily life.

Like other poets — more than other poets — with his expanding genius his ambition grew. Fountainheads, and pathless groves did not content him. It is a national sin. There is, you know, an optical distemper endemic in the city of Washington, contracted by Senators and others who once look at the President's chair; their eyes grow to it; they can never again take their eyes off it. The virus once in, is not to be got out of the system. Our friend has not this malady, but has symptoms of another,

"That last infirmity of noble minds."

Ah, gentlemen! so cold and majestic as he sits here, I hear this sin burned at his heart — well hid, I own; never was a man more modest, less boastful, less egotistical. But you remember that wicked Phidias, who, after making his divine Minerva, carved his own image with such deep incision into the shield, that it could not be effaced without destroying the statue. But this artist of ours, with deeper cunning, has contrived to levy on all American nature, has subsidized every solitary grove and monument-mountain in Berkshire or the Katskills, every gleaming water, the " gardens of the Desert," every waterfowl and woodbird, the evening wind, the stormy March, the song of the stars; — has suborned every one of these to speak for him, so that there is no feature of day or night in the country which does not, to the contemplative mind, recall the name of Bryant. This high-handed usurpation of whatever is sweet or sublime, I charge him with, and, on the top of this, with the sorcery of making us hug our fetters and rejoice in our subjugation.

Then, sir, for his patriotism — we all know the deep debt which the country owes to the accomplished journalist, who, the better to carry the ends which his heart desired, left the studies and retirements dear to his muse, adapted his voice to the masses to be reached, and the great cause to be sustained — was content to drop " the garland and singing-robes of the poet," and, masking his Tyrtaean elegies in the plain speech of the street, sounded the key-note of policy and duty to the American people, in a manner and with an effect of the highest service to the Republic.

Before I sit down, let me apply to him a verse addressed by Thomas Moore to the poet Crabbe, and Moore has written few better:

> " True bard, and simple as the race
> Of heaven-born poets always are,
> When stooping from their starry place,
> They're children, but gods afar."

ARTHUR HUGH CLOUGH

REVIEW OF THE BOTHIE OF TOPER-NA-FUOSICH, A LONG-VACATION PASTORAL, BY ARTHUR CLOUGH

HERE is a new English poem which we heartily recommend to all classes of readers. It is an account of one of those Oxford reading-parties which, at the beginning of a long vacation, are made up by a tutor with five or six undergraduates, who wish to bring up arrears of study, or to *cram* for examination and honors, and who betake themselves with their guide to some romantic spot in Wales or Scotland, where are good bathing and shooting, read six hours a day, and kill the other eighteen in sport, smoking, and sleep. The poem is as jocund and buoyant as the party, and so joyful a picture of college life and manners, with such good strokes of revenge on the old tormentors, Pindar, Thucydides, Aristotle, and the logical Aldrich, that one wonders that this ground has not been broken up before. Six young men have read three weeks with their tutor, and after joining in a country dinner and a dance in a barn, four of them decide to give up books for three weeks, and make a tour of the Highlands, leaving the other two partners with the tutor in the cottage, to their *matutive,* or morning bath, six hours' reading, and mutton at seven. The portraits of the young party are briefly but masterly sketched. Adam the tutor, Lindsay the dialectician, Hope, Hobbes, Airlie, Arthur, who, from his thirty feet diving, is the " glory of headers," and Hewson. Philip Hewson, the hero of the poem, the radical poet, in this excursion falls in love with the golden-haired Katie at the farm of Rannoch, and is left behind by his returning fellows. The poet follows his hero into the mountains, wherever the restless Philip wanders, brooding on his passion.

Whilst the tutor anxiously, and his companions more joyously, are speculating on this dubious adventure of their comrade, a letter arrives at the cottage from Hope, who travelled with Philip, announcing that Philip and Katie have parted, and that Philip is staying at Castle Balloch, in assiduous attendance on the beautiful "Lady Maria." In an earnest letter to his friend the tutor, Philip explains himself; and the free-winged sweep of speculation to which his new life at the Castle gives occasion, is in a truly modern spirit, and sufficiently embarrassing, one can see, to the friendliest of tutors. Great is the mirth of the Oxford party at this new phase of the ardent Philip, but it is suddenly checked again by a new letter from Philip to Adam, entreating him to come immediately to the *bothie* or hut of Toper-na-Fuosich, to bring him counsel and sanction, since he has already found rest and home in the heart of —— Elspie!

We are now introduced to Elspie, the right Anteros, hitherto pursued in vain under deceiving masks, and are made with Adam the tutor to acquiesce in Philip's final choice. The story leads naturally into a bold hypothetical discussion of the most serious questions that bubble up at this very hour in London, Paris, and Boston, and, whilst these are met and honestly and even profoundly treated, the dialogue charms us by perfect good breeding and exuberant animal spirits. We shall not say that the rapid and bold execution has the finish and the intimate music we demand in modern poetry; but the subject-matter is so solid, and the figures so real and lifelike, that the poem is justified, and would be good in spite of much ruder execution than we here find. Yet the poem has great literary merits. The author has a true eye for nature, and expresses himself through the justest images. The Homeric iteration has a singular charm, half-comic, half-poetic, in the piece, and there is a wealth of expression, a power of description and of portrait-painting, which excels our best romancers. Even the hexameter, which with all our envy of its beauty in Latin and in Greek, we think not agreeable to the genius of English poetry, is here in place to heighten the humor of college conversation.

CARLYLE'S FRENCH REVOLUTION

A REVIEW IN THE CHRISTIAN EXAMINER, JANUARY, 1838

We welcome the appearance in this country of this extraordinary work. It is by far the largest, the most elaborate, and the best work which Mr. Carlyle has yet attempted, and although an accurate and extended history, not a whit less original and eccentric than any of his earlier productions. One thing has for some time been becoming plainer, and is now quite undeniable, that Mr. Carlyle's genius, whether benignant or baleful, is no transient meteor, and no expiring taper, but a robust flame self-kindled and self-fed, and more likely to light others into a conflagration, than to be speedily blown out. The work before us indicates an extent of resources, a power of labor, and powers of thought, seldom combined, and never without permanent effects.

It is a part of Mr. Carlyle's literary creed, "that all history is poetry, were it rightly told." The work before us is his own exemplification of his doctrine. The poetry consists in the historian's point of view. With the most accurate and lively delineation of the crowded actions of the revolution, there is the constant co-perception of the universal relations of each man. With a painter's eye for picturesque groups, and a boy's passion for exciting details, he combines a philosopher's habitual wonder as he stands before the insoluble mysteries of the Advent and Death of man.

From this point of view, he is unable to part, and the noble and hopeful heart of the narrator breathes a music of humanity through every part of the tale. Always equal to his subject, he has first thought it through; and having seen in the sequence of events the illustration of high and beautiful laws which exist eternal in the reason of man, he beholds calmly like a god the fury of the action, secure in his own perception of the general harmony resulting from particular horror or pain. This elevation of the historian's point of view is not, however, produced at any expense of attention to details. Here is a chronicle as minute as Froissart, and a scrupulous weighing of historical evidence, which begets implicit trust. Above all, we have men in the story, and not names merely. The characters are so sharply drawn that they cannot be confounded or forgotten, though we may sometimes doubt whether the thrilling impersonation is in very deed the historic man whose name it bears.

We confess we feel much curiosity in regard to the immediate success of this bold and original experiment upon the public taste. It seems very certain that the chasm which existed in English literature, the want of a just history of the French Revolution, is now filled in a manner to prevent all competition. But how far Mr. Carlyle's manifold innovations shall be reckoned worthy of adoption and of emulation, or what portion of them shall remain to himself incommunicable, as the anomalies of a genius too self-indulgent, time alone can show.

PAPERS FROM THE DIAL

PAPERS FROM THE DIAL

THE EDITORS TO THE READER

INTRODUCTION TO THE FIRST ISSUE OF THE DIAL, JULY, 1840

We invite the attention of our countrymen to a new design. Probably not quite unexpected or unannounced will our Journal appear, though small pains have been taken to secure its welcome. Those, who have immediately acted in editing the present Number, cannot accuse themselves of any unbecoming forwardness in their undertaking, but rather of a backwardness, when they remember how often in many private circles the work was projected, how eagerly desired, and only postponed because no individual volunteered to combine and concentrate the free-will offerings of many coöperators. With some reluctance the present conductors of this work have yielded themselves to the wishes of their friends, finding something sacred and not to be withstood in the importunity which urged the production of a Journal in a new spirit.

As they have not proposed themselves to the work, neither can they lay any the least claim to an option or determination of the spirit in which it is conceived, or to what is peculiar in the design. In that respect, they have obeyed, though with great joy, the strong current of thought and feeling, which, for a few years past, has led many sincere persons in New England to make new demands on literature, and to reprobate that rigor of our conventions of religion and education which is turning us to stone, which renounces hope, which looks only backward, which asks only such a future as the past, which suspects improvement, and holds nothing so much in horror as new views and the dreams of youth.

With these terrors the conductors of the present Journal have nothing to do, — not even so much as a word of reproach to waste. They know that there is a portion of the youth and of the adult population of this country, who have not shared them; who have in secret or in public paid their vows to truth and freedom; who love reality too well to care for names, and who live by a Faith too earnest and profound to suffer them to doubt the eternity of its object, or to shake themselves free from its authority. Under the fictions and customs which occupied others, these have explored the Necessary, the Plain, the True, the Human, — and so gained a vantage ground, which commands the history of the past and the present.

No one can converse much with different classes of society in New England, without remarking the progress of a revolution. Those who share in it have no external organization, no badge, no creed, no name. They do not vote, or print, or even meet together. They do not know each other's faces or names. They are united only in a common love of truth, and love of its work. They are of all conditions and constitutions. Of these acolytes, if some are happily born and well bred, many are no doubt ill dressed, ill placed, ill made — with as many scars of hereditary vice as other men. Without pomp, without trumpet, in lonely and obscure places, in solitude, in servitude, in compunctions and privations, trudging beside the team in the dusty road, or drudging a hireling in other men's cornfields, schoolmasters, who teach a few children rudiments for a pittance, ministers of small parishes of the obscurer sects, lone women in dependent condition, matrons and young maidens, rich and poor, beautiful and hard-favored, without concert or proclamation of any kind, they have silently given in their several adherence to a new hope, and in all companies do signify a greater trust in the nature and resources of man, than the laws or the popular opinions will well allow.

This spirit of the time is felt by every individual with some difference, — to each one casting its light upon the objects nearest to his temper and habits of thought; — to one, coming in the shape of special reforms in the state; to another, in modifications of the various callings of men, and the customs of business; to a third, opening a new scope for literature and art; to a fourth, in philosophical insight; to a fifth, in the vast solitudes of prayer. It is in every form a protest against usage, and a search for principles. In all its movements, it is peaceable, and in the very lowest marked with a triumphant success. Of course, it rouses the opposition of all which it judges and condemns, but it is too confident in its tone to comprehend an objection, and so builds no outworks for possible defence against contingent enemies. It has the step of Fate, and goes on existing like an oak or a river, because it must.

In literature, this influence appears not yet in new books so much as in the higher tone of criticism. The antidote to all narrowness is the comparison of the record with nature, which at once shames the record and stimulates to new attempts. Whilst we look at this, we wonder how any book has been thought worthy to be preserved. There is somewhat in all life untranslatable into language. He who keeps his eye on that will write better than others, and think less of his writing, and of all writing. Every thought has a certain imprisoning as well as uplifting quality, and, in proportion to its energy on the will, refuses to become an object of intellectual contemplation. Thus what is great usually slips through our fingers, and it seems wonderful how a lifelike word ever comes to be written. If our Journal share the impulses of the time, it cannot now prescribe its own course. It cannot foretell in orderly propositions what it shall attempt. All criticism should be poetic; unpredictable; superseding, as every new thought does, all foregone thoughts, and making a new light on the whole world. Its brow is not wrinkled with circumspection, but serene, cheerful, adoring. It has all things to say, and no less than all the world for its final audience.

Our plan embraces much more than criticism; were it not so, our criticism would be naught. Everything noble is directed on life, and this is. We do not wish to say pretty or curious things, or to reiterate a few propositions in varied forms, but, if we can, to give expression to that spirit which lifts men to a higher platform, restores to them the religious sentiment, brings them worthy aims and pure pleasures, purges the inward eye, makes life less desultory, and, through raising man to the level of nature, takes away its melancholy from the landscape, and reconciles the practical with the speculative powers.

But perhaps we are telling our little story too gravely. There are always great arguments at hand for a true action, even for the writing of a few pages. There is nothing but seems near it and prompts it, — the sphere in the ecliptic, the sap in the apple tree, — every fact, every appearance seem to persuade to it.

Our means correspond with the ends we have indicated. As we wish not to multiply books, but to report life, our resources are therefore not so much the pens of practised writers, as the discourse of the living, and the portfolios which friendship has opened to us. From the beautiful recesses of private thought; from the experience and hope of spirits which are withdrawing from all old forms, and seeking in all that is new somewhat to meet their inappeasable longings; from the secret confession of genius afraid to trust itself to aught but sympathy; from the conversation of fervid and mystical pietists; from tear-stained diaries of sorrow and passion; from the manuscripts of young poets; and from the records of youthful taste commenting on old works of art; we hope to draw thoughts and feelings, which being alive can impart life.

And so with diligent hands and good intent we set down our Dial on the earth. We wish it may resemble that instrument in its celebrated happiness, that of measuring no hours but those of sunshine. Let it be one cheerful rational voice amidst the din of mourners and polemics. Or to abide by our chosen image, let it be such a Dial, not as the dead face of a clock, hardly even such as the Gnomon in a garden, but rather such a Dial as is the Garden itself, in whose leaves and flowers and fruits the suddenly awakened sleeper is instantly apprised not what part of dead time, but what state of life and growth is now arrived and arriving.

THOUGHTS ON ART

JANUARY, 1841

Every department of life at the present day, — Trade, Politics, Letters, Science, Religion, — seem to feel, and to labor to express the identity of their law. They are rays of one sun; they translate each into a new language the sense of the other. They are sublime when seen as emanations of a Necessity contradistinguished from the vulgar Fate, by being instant and alive, and dissolving man as well as his works, in its flowing beneficence. This influence is conspicuously visible in the principles and history of Art.

On one side, in primary communication with absolute truth, through thought and instinct, the human mind tends by an equal necessity, on the other side, to the publication and embodiment of its thought, — modified and dwarfed by the impurity and untruth which, in all our experience, injures the wonderful medium through which it passes. The child not only suffers, but cries; not only hungers, but eats. The man not only thinks, but speaks and acts. Every thought that arises in the mind, in its rising, aims to pass out of the mind into act; just as every plant, in the moment of germination, struggles up to light. Thought is the seed of action; but action is as much its second form as thought is its first. It rises in thought to the end, that it may be uttered and acted. The more profound the thought, the more burdensome. Always in proportion to the depth of its sense does it knock importunately at the gates of the soul, to be spoken, to be done. What is in, will out. It struggles to the birth. Speech is a great pleasure, and action a great pleasure; they cannot be forborne.

The utterance of thought and emotion in speech and action may be conscious or unconscious. The sucking child is an unconscious actor. A man in an ecstasy of fear or anger is an unconscious actor. A large part of our habitual actions are unconsciously done, and most of our necessary words are unconsciously said.

The conscious utterance of thought, by speech or action, to any end, is Art. From the first imitative babble of a child to the despotism of eloquence; from his first pile of toys or chip bridge, to the masonry of Eddystone lighthouse or the Erie canal; from the tattooing of the Owhyhees to the Vatican Gallery; from the simplest expedient of private prudence to the American Constitution; from its first to its last works, Art is the spirit's voluntary use and combination of things to serve its end. The Will distinguishes it as spiritual action. Relatively to themselves, the bee, the bird, the beaver, have no art, for what they do, they do instinctively; but relatively to the Supreme Being, they have. And the same is true of all unconscious action; relatively to the doer, it is instinct; relatively to the First Cause, it is Art. In this sense, recognizing the Spirit which informs Nature, Plato rightly said, " Those things which are said to be done by Nature, are indeed done by Divine Art." Art, universally, is the spirit creative. It was defined by Aristotle, " The reason of the thing, without the matter," as he defined the art of ship-building to be, " All of the ship but the wood."

If we follow the popular distinction of works according to their aim, we should say, the Spirit, in its creation, aims at use or at beauty, and hence Art divides itself into the Useful and the Fine Arts.

The useful arts comprehend not only those that lie next to instinct, as agriculture, building, weaving, &c., but also navigation, practical chemistry, and the construction of all the grand and delicate tools and instruments by which man serves himself; as language; the watch; the ship; the decimal cipher; and also the sciences, so far as they are made serviceable to political economy.

The moment we begin to reflect on the pleasure we receive from a ship, a railroad, a dry dock; or from a picture, a dramatic representation, a statue, a poem, we find that they have not a quite simple, but a blended origin. We find that the question, — What is Art? leads us directly to another, — Who is the artist? and the solution of this is the key to the history of Art.

I hasten to state the principle which prescribes, through different means, its firm law to the useful and the beautiful arts. The law is this. The universal soul is the alone creator of the useful and the beautiful; therefore to make anything useful or beautiful, the individual must be submitted to the universal mind.

In the first place, let us consider this in reference to the useful arts. Here the omnipotent agent is Nature; all human acts are satellites to her orb. Nature is the representative of the universal mind, and the law becomes this, — that Art must be a complement to nature, strictly subsidiary. It was said, in allusion to the great structures of the ancient Romans, the aqueducts and bridges, — that their "Art was a Nature working to municipal ends." That is a true account of all just works of useful art. Smeaton built Eddystone lighthouse on the model of an oak tree, as being the form in nature best designed to resist a constant assailing force. Dollond formed his achromatic telescope on the model of the human eye. Duhamel built a bridge, by letting in a piece of stronger timber for the middle of the under surface, getting his hint from the structure of the shin-bone.

The first and last lesson of the useful arts is, that nature tyrannizes over our works. They must be conformed to her law, or they will be ground to powder by her omnipresent activity. Nothing droll, nothing whimsical will endure. Nature is ever interfering with Art. You cannot build your house or pagoda as you will, but as you must. There is a quick bound set to our caprice. The leaning tower can only lean so far. The verandah or pagoda roof can curve upward only to a certain point. The slope of your roof is determined by the weight of snow. It is only within narrow limits that the discretion of the architect may range. Gravity, wind, sun, rain, the size of men and animals, and such like, have more to say than he. It is the law of fluids that prescribes the shape of the boat, — keel, rudder, and bows, — and, in the finer fluid above, the form and tackle of the sails. Man seems to have no option about his tools, but merely the necessity to learn from Nature what will fit best, as if he were fitting a screw or a door. Beneath a necessity thus almighty, what is artificial in man's life seems insignificant. He seems to take his task so minutely from intimations of Nature, that his works become as it were hers, and he is no longer free.

But if we work within this limit, she yields us all her strength. All powerful action is performed, by bringing the forces of nature to bear upon our objects. We do not grind corn or lift the loom by our own strength, but we build a mill in such a position as to set the north wind to play upon our instrument, or the elastic force of steam, or the ebb and flow of the sea. So in our handiwork, we do few things by muscular force, but we place ourselves in such attitudes as to bring the force of gravity, that is, the weight of the planet, to bear upon the spade or the axe we wield. What is it that gives force to the blow of the axe or crowbar? Is it the muscles of the laborer's arm, or is it the attraction of the whole globe below it, on the axe or bar? In short, in all our operations we seek not to use our own, but to bring a quite infinite force to bear.

Let us now consider this law as it affects the works that have beauty for their end, that is, the productions of the Fine Arts.

Here again the prominent fact is subordination of man. His art is the least part of his work of art. A great deduction is to be made before we can know his proper contribution to it.

Music, eloquence, poetry, painting, sculpture, architecture. This is a rough enumeration of the Fine Arts. I omit rhetoric, which only respects the form of eloquence and poetry. Architecture and eloquence are mixed arts, whose end is sometimes beauty and sometimes use.

It will be seen that in each of these arts there is much which is not spiritual. Each has a material basis, and in each the creating intellect is crippled in some degree by the stuff on which it works. The basis of poetry is language, which is material only on one side. It is a demi-god. But being applied primarily to the common necessities of man, it is not new created by the poet for his own ends.

The basis of music is the qualities of the air and the vibrations of sonorous bodies. The pulsation of a stretched string or wire, gives the ear the pleasure of sweet sound, before yet the musician has enhanced this pleasure by concords and combinations.

Eloquence, as far as it is a fine art, is modified how much by the material organization of the orator, the tone of the voice, the physical strength, the play of the eye and countenance! All this is so much deduction from the purely spiritual pleasure. All this is so much deduction from the merit of Art, and is the attribute of Nature.

In painting, bright colors stimulate the eye, before yet they are harmonized into a landscape. In sculpture and in architecture, the material, as marble or granite; and in architecture, the mass, — are sources of great pleasure, quite independent of the artificial arrangement. The art resides in the model, in the plan, for it is on that the genius of the artist is expended, not on the statue, or the temple. Just as much better as is the polished statue of dazzling marble than the clay model; or as much more impressive as is the granite cathedral or pyramid than the ground-plan or profile of them on paper, so much more beauty owe they to Nature than to Art.

There is a still larger deduction to be made from the genius of the artist in favor of Nature than I have yet specified.

A jumble of musical sounds on a viol or a flute, in which the rhythm of the tune is played without one of the notes being right, gives pleasure to the unskilful ear. A very coarse imitation of the human form on canvas, or in wax-work, — a very coarse sketch in colors of a landscape, in which imitation is all that is attempted, — these things give to unpractised eyes, to the uncultured, who do not ask a fine spiritual delight, almost as much pleasure as a statue of Canova or a picture of Titian.

And in the statue of Canova, or the picture of

Titian, these give the great part of the pleasure; they are the basis on which the fine spirit rears a higher delight, but to which these are indispensable.

Another deduction from the genius of the artist is what is conventional in his art, of which there is much in every work of art. Thus how much is there that is not original in every particular building, in every statue, in every tune, in every painting, in every poem, in every harangue. Whatever is national or usual; as the usage of building all Roman churches in the form of a cross, the prescribed distribution of parts of a theatre, the custom of draping a statue in classical costume. Yet who will deny that the merely conventional part of the performance contributes much to its effect?

One consideration more exhausts, I believe, all the deductions from the genius of the artist in any given work.

This is the adventitious. Thus the pleasure that a noble temple gives us, is only in part owing to the temple. It is exalted by the beauty of sunlight, by the play of the clouds, by the landscape around it, by its grouping with the houses, and trees, and towers, in its vicinity. The pleasure of eloquence is in greatest part owing often to the stimulus of the occasion which produces it; to the magic of sympathy, which exalts the feeling of each, by radiating on him the feeling of all.

The effect of music belongs how much to the place, as the church, or the moonlight walk, or to the company, or, if on the stage, to what went before in the play, or to the expectation of what shall come after.

In poetry, " It is tradition more than invention helps the poet to a good fable." The adventitious beauty of poetry may be felt in the greater delight which a verse gives in happy quotation than in the poem.

It is a curious proof of our conviction that the artist does not feel himself to be the parent of his work and is as much surprised at the effect as we, that we are so unwilling to impute our best sense of any work of art to the author. The very highest praise we can attribute to any writer, painter, sculptor, builder, is, that he actually possessed the thought or feeling with which he has inspired us. We hesitate at doing Spenser so great an honor as to think that he intended by his allegory the sense we affix to it. We grudge to Homer the wise human circumspection his commentators ascribe to him. Even Shakspeare, of whom we can believe everything, we think indebted to Goethe and to Coleridge for the wisdom they detect in his Hamlet and Anthony. Especially have we this infirmity of faith in contemporary genius. We fear that Allston and Greenough did not foresee and design all the effect they produce on us.

Our arts are happy hits. We are like the musician on the lake, whose melody is sweeter than he knows, or like a traveller, surprised by a mountain echo, whose trivial word returns to him in romantic thunders.

In view of these facts, I say that the power of Nature predominates over the human will in all works of even the fine arts, in all that respects their material and external circumstances. Nature paints the best part of the picture; carves the best part of the statue; builds the best part of the house; and speaks the best part of the oration. For all the advantages to which I have adverted are such as the artist did not consciously produce. He relied on their aid, he put himself in the way to receive aid from some of them, but he saw that his planting and his watering waited for the sunlight of Nature, or was vain.

Let us proceed to the consideration of the great law stated in the beginning of this essay, as it affects the purely spiritual part of a work of art.

As in useful art, so far as it is useful, the work must be strictly subordinated to the laws of Nature, so as to become a sort of continuation, and in no wise a contradiction of Nature; so in art that aims at beauty as an end, must the parts be subordinated to Ideal Nature, and everything individual abstracted, so that it shall be the production of the universal soul.

The artist, who is to produce a work which is to be admired not by his friends or his townspeople, or his contemporaries, but by all men; and which is to be more beautiful to the eye in proportion to its culture, must disindividualize himself, and be a man of no party, and no manner, and no age, but one through whom the soul of all men circulates, as the common air through his lungs. He must work in the spirit in which we conceive a prophet to speak, or an angel of the Lord to act, that is, he is not to speak his own words, or do his own works, or think his own thoughts, but he is to be an organ through which the universal mind acts.

In speaking of the useful arts, I pointed to the fact, that we do not dig, or grind, or hew, by our muscular strength, but by bringing the weight of the planet to bear on the spade, axe, or bar. Precisely analogous to this, in the fine arts, is the manner of our intellectual work. We aim to hinder our individuality from acting. So much as we can shove aside our egotism, our prejudice, and will, and bring the omniscience of reason upon the subject before us, so perfect is the work. The wonders of Shakspeare are things which he saw whilst he stood aside, and then returned to record them. The poet aims at getting observations without aim; to subject to thought things seen without (voluntary) thought.

In eloquence, the great triumphs of the art are, when the orator is lifted above himself; when consciously he makes himself the mere tongue of the occasion and the hour, and says what cannot but be said. Hence the French phrase *l'abandon,* to describe the self-surrender of the orator. Not his will, but the principle on which he is horsed, the great connection and crisis of events thunder in the ear of the crowd.

In poetry, where every word is free, every word is necessary. Good poetry could not have been otherwise written than it is. The first time you hear it, it sounds rather as if copied out of some invisible tablet in the Eternal mind, than as if arbitrarily composed by the poet. The feeling of all great poets has accorded with this. They found the verse, not made it. The muse brought it to them.

In sculpture, did ever anybody call the Apollo a fancy piece? Or say of the Laocoön how it might be made different? A masterpiece of art has in the mind a fixed place in the chain of being, as much as a plant or a crystal.

The whole language of men, especially of artists, in reference to this subject, points at the belief, that every work of art, in proportion to its excellence, partakes of the precision of fate; no room was there for choice; no play for fancy; for the moment, or in the successive moments, when that form was seen, the iron lids of Reason were unclosed, which ordinarily are heavy with slumber: that the individual mind became for the moment the vent of the mind of humanity.

There is but one Reason. The mind that made the world is not one mind, but *the* mind. Every man is an inlet to the same, and to all of the same. And every work of art is a more or less pure manifestation of the same. Therefore we arrive at this conclusion, which I offer as a confirmation of the whole view: That the delight, which a work of art affords, seems to arise from our recognizing in it the mind that formed Nature again in active operation.

It differs from the works of Nature in this, that they are organically reproductive. This is not: but spiritually it is prolific by its powerful action on the intellects of men.

In confirmation of this view, let me refer to the fact, that a study of admirable works of art always sharpens the perceptions of the beauty of Nature; that a certain analogy reigns throughout the wonders of both; that the contemplation of a work of great art draws us into a state of mind which may be called religious. It conspires with all exalted sentiments.

Proceeding from absolute mind, whose nature is goodness as much as truth, they are always attuned to moral nature. If the earth and sea conspire with virtue more than vice, — so do the masterpieces of art. The galleries of ancient sculpture in Naples and Rome strike no deeper conviction into the mind than the contrast of the purity, the severity, expressed in these fine old heads, with the frivolity and grossness of the mob that exhibits, and the mob that gazes at them. These are the countenances of the first-born, the face of man in the morning of the world. No mark is on these lofty features of sloth, or luxury, or meanness, and they surprise you with a moral admonition, as they speak of nothing around you, but remind you of the fragrant thoughts and the purest resolutions of your youth.

Herein is the explanation of the analogies which exist in all the arts. They are the reappearance of one mind, working in many materials to many temporary ends. Raphael paints wisdom; Handel sings it, Phidias carves it, Shakspeare writes it, Wren builds it, Columbus sails it, Luther preaches it, Washington arms it, Watt mechanizes it. Painting was called "silent poetry;" and poetry "speaking painting." The laws of each art are convertible into the laws of every other.

Herein we have an explanation of the necessity that reigns in all the kingdom of art.

Arising out of eternal reason, one and perfect, whatever is beautiful rests on the foundation of the necessary. Nothing is arbitrary, nothing is insulated in beauty. It depends forever on the necessary and the useful. The plumage of the bird, the mimic plumage of the insect, has a reason for its rich colors in the constitution of the animal. Fitness is so inseparable an accompaniment of beauty, that it has been taken for it. The most perfect form to answer an end, is so far beautiful. In the mind of the artist, could we enter there, we should see the sufficient reason for the last flourish and tendril of his work, just as every tint and spine in the sea-shell preëxists in the secreting organs of the fish. We feel, in seeing a noble building, which rhymes well, as we do in hearing a perfect song, that it is spiritually organic, that is, had a necessity in nature, for being, was one of the possible forms in the Divine mind, and is now only discovered and executed by the artist, not arbitrarily composed by him.

And so every genuine work of art has as much reason for being as the earth and the sun. The gayest charm of beauty has a root in the constitution of things. The Iliad of Homer, the songs of David, the odes of Pindar, the tragedies of Æschylus, the Doric temples, the Gothic cathedrals, the plays of

Shakspeare, were all made not for sport, but in grave earnest, in tears, and smiles of suffering and loving men.

Viewed from this point, the history of Art becomes intelligible, and, moreover, one of the most agreeable studies in the world. We see how each work of art sprang irresistibly from necessity, and, moreover, took its form from the broad hint of Nature. Beautiful in this wise is the obvious origin of all the known orders of architecture, namely, that they were the idealizing of the primitive abodes of each people. Thus the Doric temple still presents the semblance of the wooden cabin, in which the Dorians dwelt. The Chinese pagoda is plainly a Tartar tent. The Indian and Egyptian temples still betray the mounds and subterranean houses of their forefathers. The Gothic church plainly originated in a rude adaptation of forest trees, with their boughs on, to a festal or solemn edifice, as the bands around the cleft pillars still indicate the green withs that tied them. No one can walk in a pine barren, in one of the paths which the woodcutters make for their teams, without being struck with the architectural appearance of the grove, especially in winter, when the bareness of all other trees shows the low arch of the Saxons. In the woods, in a winter afternoon, one will see as readily the origin of the stained glass window with which the Gothic cathedrals are adorned, in the colors of the western sky, seen through the bare and crossing branches of the forest. Nor, I think, can any lover of nature enter the old piles of Oxford and the English cathedrals, without feeling that the forest overpowered the mind of the builder, with its ferns, its spikes of flowers, its locust, its oak, its pine, its fir, its spruce. The cathedral is a blossoming in stone, subdued by the insatiable demand of harmony in man.

The mountain of granite blooms into an eternal flower, with the lightness and delicate finish, as well as aerial proportions and perspective of vegetable beauty.

There was no wilfulness in the savages in this perpetuating of their first rude abodes. The first form in which they built a house would be the first form of their public and religious edifice also. This form becomes immediately sacred in the eyes of their children, and the more so, as more traditions cluster round it, and is, therefore, imitated with more splendor in each succeeding generation.

In like manner, it has been remarked by Goethe, that the granite breaks into parallelopipeds, which, broken in two, one part would be an obelisk; that in Upper Egypt the inhabitants would naturally mark a memorable spot by setting up so conspicuous a stone. Again, he suggested we may see in any stone wall, on a fragment of rock, the projecting veins of harder stone, which have resisted the action of frost and water, which has decomposed the rest. This appearance certainly gave the hint of the hieroglyphics inscribed on their obelisk. The amphitheatre of the old Romans, — any one may see its origin, who looks at the crowd running together to see any fight, sickness, or odd appearance in the street. The first comers gather round in a circle; those behind stand on tiptoe; and further back they climb on fences or window sills, and so make a cup of which the object of attention occupies the hollow area. The architect put benches in this order, and enclosed the cup with a wall, and behold a coliseum.

It would be easy to show of very many fine things in the world, in the customs of nations, the etiquette of courts, the constitution of governments, the origin in very simple local necessities. Heraldry, for example, and the ceremonies of a coronation, are a splendid burlesque of the occurrences that might befal a dragoon and his footboy. The College of Cardinals were originally the parish priests of Rome. The leaning towers originated from the civil discords which induced every lord to build a tower. Then it became a point of family pride, — and for pride a leaning tower was built.

This strict dependence of art upon material and ideal nature, this adamantine necessity, which it underlies, has made all its past, and may foreshow its future history. It never was in the power of any man, or any community, to call the arts into being. They come to serve his actual wants, never to please his fancy. These arts have their origin always in some enthusiasm, as love, patriotism, or religion. Who carved marble? The believing man, who wished to symbolize their gods to the waiting Greeks.

The Gothic cathedrals were built, when the builder and the priest and the people were overpowered by their faith. Love and fear laid every stone. The Madonnas of Raphael and Titian were made to be worshipped. Tragedy was instituted for the like purpose, and the miracles of music; — all sprang out of some genuine enthusiasm, and never out of dilettantism and holidays. But now they languish, because their purpose is merely exhibition. Who cares, who knows what works of art our government have ordered to be made for the capitol? They are a mere flourish to please the eye of persons who have associations with books and galleries. But in Greece, the Demos of Athens divided into political factions upon the merits of Phidias.

In this country, at this time, other interests than religion and patriotism are predominant, and the arts, the daughters of enthusiasm, do not flourish.

The genuine offspring of our ruling passions we behold. Popular institutions, the school, the reading room, the post office, the exchange, the insurance company, and an immense harvest of economical inventions, are the fruit of the equality and the boundless liberty of lucrative callings. These are superficial wants; and their fruits are these superficial institutions. But as far as they accelerate the end of political freedom and national education, they are preparing the soil of man for fairer flowers and fruits in another age. For beauty, truth, and goodness are not obsolete; they spring eternal in the breast of man; they are as indigenous in Massachusetts as in Tuscany, or the Isles of Greece. And that Eternal Spirit, whose triple face they are, moulds from them forever, for his mortal child, images to remind him of the Infinite and Fair.

THE SENSES AND THE SOUL

JANUARY, 1842

"WHAT we know is a point to what we do not know." The first questions are still to be asked. Let any man bestow a thought on himself, how he came hither, and whither he tends, and he will find that all the literature, all the philosophy that is on record, have done little to dull the edge of inquiry. The globe that swims so silently with us through the sea of space, has never a port, but with its little convoy of friendly orbs pursues its voyage through the signs of heaven, to renew its navigation again forever. The wonderful tidings our glasses and calendars give us concerning the hospitable lights that hang around us in the deep, do not appease but inflame our curiosity; and in like manner, our culture does not lead to any goal, but its richest results of thought and action are only new preparation.

Here on the surface of our swimming earth we come out of silence into society already formed, into language, customs, and traditions, ready made, and the multitude of our associates discountenance us from expressing any surprise at the somewhat agreeable novelty of Being, and frown down any intimation on our part of a disposition to assume our own vows, to preserve our independence, and to institute any inquiry into the sweet and sublime vision which surrounds us.

And yet there seems no need that any should fear we should grow too wise. The path of truth has obstacles enough of its own. We dwell on the surface of nature. We dwell amidst surfaces; and surface laps so closely on surface, that we cannot easily pierce to see the interior organism. Then the subtlety of things! Under every cause, another cause. Truth soars too high or dives too deep for the most resolute inquirer. See of how much we know nothing. See the strange position of man. Our science neither comprehends him as a whole, nor any one of its particulars. See the action and reaction of Will and Necessity. See his passions, and their origin in the deeps of nature and circumstance. See the Fear that rides even the brave. See the omnipresent Hope, whose fountains in our consciousness no metaphysician can find. Consider the phenomenon of Laughter, and explore the elements of the Comic. What do we know of the mystery of Music? and what of Form? why this stroke, this outline should express beauty, and that other not? See the occult region of Demonology, with coincidence, foresight, dreams, and omens. Consider the appearance of Death, the formidable secret of our destiny, looming up as the barrier of nature.

Our ignorance is great enough, and yet the fact most surprising is not our ignorance, but the aversation of men from knowledge. That which, one would say, would unite all minds and join all hands, the ambition to push as far as fate would permit, the planted garden of man on every hand into the kingdom of Night, really fires the heart of few and solitary men. Tell men to study themselves, and for the most part, they find nothing less interesting. Whilst we walk environed before and behind with Will, Fate, Hope, Fear, Love, and Death, these phantoms or angels, whom we catch at but cannot embrace, it is droll to see the contentment and incuriosity of man. All take for granted, — the learned as well as the unlearned, — that a great deal, nay, almost all, is known and forever settled. But in truth all is now to be begun, and every new mind ought to take the attitude of Columbus, launch out from the gaping loiterers on the shore, and sail west for a new world.

This profound ignorance, this deep sleep of the higher faculties of man, coexists with a great abundance of what are called the means of learning, great activity of book-making, and of formal teaching. Go into one of our public libraries, when a new box of books and journals has arrived with the usual importation of the periodical literature of England. The best names of Britain are on the covers. What a mass of literary production for a single week or month! We speculate upon it before we read. We say, what an invention is the press and the journal, by which a hundred pale students, each a hive of distilled flowers of learning, of thought, — each a poet, — each an accomplished man whom the selectest influences have joined to breed and enrich, are made to unite their manifold streams for the information and delight of everybody who can read! How lame is speech, how imperfect the communication of the ancient Harper, wandering from castle to hamlet, to sing to a vagrant audience his melodious thoughts! These unopened books contain the chosen verses of a hundred minstrels, born, living, and singing in distant countries and different languages; for, the intellectual wealth of the world, like its commercial, rolls to London, and through that great heart is hurled again to the extremities. And here, too, is the result, not poetic, of how much thought, how much experience, and how much suffering of wise and cultivated men! How can we in America expect books of our own, whilst this bale of wisdom arrives once or twice in a month at our ports?

In this mind we open the books, and begin to read. We find they are books about books; and then perhaps the book criticized was itself a compilation or digest of others; so that the page we read is at third or fourth hand from the event or sentiment which it describes. Then we find that much the largest proportion of the pages relates exclusively to matter of fact — to the superficial fact, and, as if systematically, shuns any reference to a thought or law which the fact indicated. A large part again, both of the prose and verse, is gleanings from old compositions, and the oft repeated praise of such is repeated in the phrase of the present day. We have even the mortification to find one more deduction still from our anticipated prize, namely, that a large portion of ostentatious criticism is merely a hired advertisement of the great booksellers. In the course of our turning of leaves, we fall at last on an extraordinary passage — a record of thought and virtue, or a clarion strain of poetry, or perchance a traveller makes us acquainted with strange modes of life and some relic of primeval religion, or, rarer yet, a profound sentence is here printed — shines here new but eternal on these linen pages, — we wonder whence it came, — or perhaps trace it instantly home — *aut Erasmus aut Diabolus* — to the only head it could come from.

A few thoughts are all we glean from the best inspection of the paper pile; all the rest is combination and confectionary. A little part abides in our memory, and goes to exalt the sense of duty, and make us happier. For the rest, our heated expectation is chilled and disappointed. Some indirect benefit will no doubt accrue. If we read with braced and active mind, we learn this negative fact, itself a piece of human life. We contrast this mountain of dross with the grains of gold, — we oversee the writer, and learn somewhat of the laws of writing. But a lesson as good we might be learning elsewhere.

Now what is true of a month's or a year's issue of new books, seems to me with a little qualification true of the age. The *stock-writers,* (for the honesty of the literary class has given this population a name,) vastly outnumber the thinking men. One man, two men, — possibly, three or four, — have cast behind them the long-descended costume of the academy, and the expectations of fashion, and have said, This world is too fair, this world comes home too near to me than that I should walk a stranger in it, and live at second-hand, fed by other men's doctrines, or treading only in their steps; I feel a higher right herein, and will hearken to the Oracle myself. Such have perceived the extreme poverty of literature, have seen that there was not and could not be help for the fervent soul, except through its own energy. But the great number of those who have voluminously ministered to the popular tastes were men of talents, who had some feat which each could do with words, but who have not added to wisdom or to virtue. Talent amuses; Wisdom instructs. Talent shows me what another man can do; Genius acquaints me with the spacious circuits of the common nature. One is carpentry; the other is growth. To make a step into the world of thought is now given to but few men; to make a second step beyond the first, only one in a country can do; but to carry the thought on to three steps, marks a great teacher. Aladdin's palace with its one unfinished window, which all the gems in the royal treasury cannot finish in the style of the meanest of the profusion of jewelled windows that were built by the Genie in a night, is but too true an image of the efforts of talent to add one verse to the copious text which inspiration writes by one or another scribe from age to age.

It is not that the literary class or those for whom they write, are not lovers of truth, and amenable to principles. All are so. The hunger of men for truth is immense; but they are not erect on their feet; the senses are too strong for the soul. Our senses barbarize us. When the ideal world recedes before the senses, we are on a retrograde march. The savage surrenders to his senses; he is subject to paroxysms of joy and fear; he is lewd, and a drunkard. The Esquimaux in the exhilaration of the morning sun, when he is invigorated by sleep, will sell his bed. He is the fool of the moment's sensations to the degree of losing sight of the whole amount of his sensations in so many years. And there is an Esquimaux in every man which makes us believe in the permanence of this moment's state of our game more than our own experience will warrant. In the fine day we despise the house. At sea, the passengers always judge from the weather of the present moment of the probable length of the voyage. In a fresh breeze, they are sure of a good run; becalmed, they are equally sure of a long passage. In trade, the momentary state of the markets betrays continually the experienced and long-sighted. In politics, and in our opinion of the prospects of society, we are in like manner the slaves of the hour. Meet one or two malignant declaimers, and we are weary of life, and distrust the permanence of good institutions. A single man in a ragged coat at an election looks revolutionary. But ride in a stage-coach with one or two benevolent persons in good spirits, and the Republic seems to us safe.

It is but an extension of the despotism of sense, —

shall I say, only a calculated sensuality, — a little more comprehensive devotion which subjugates the eminent and the reputed wise, and hinders an ideal culture. In the great stakes which the leaders of society esteem not at all fanciful but solid, in the best reputed professions and operations, what is there which will bear the scrutiny of reason? The most active lives have so much routine as to preclude progress almost equally with the most inactive. We defer to the noted merchants whose influence is felt not only in their native cities, but in most parts of the globe; but our respect does them and ourselves great injustice, for their trade is without system, their affairs unfold themselves after no law of the mind; but are bubble built on bubble without end; a work of arithmetic, not of commerce, much less of considerate humanity. They add voyage to voyage, and buy stocks that they may buy stocks, and no ulterior purpose is thought of. When you see their dexterity in particulars, you cannot overestimate the resources of good sense, and when you find how empty they are of all remote aims, you cannot underestimate their philosophy.

The men of letters and the professions we have charged with the like surrender to routine. It is no otherwise with the men of office. Statesmen are solitary. At no time do they form a class. Governments, for the most part, are carried on by political merchants quite without principle, and according to the maxims of trade and huckster; so that what is true of merchants is true of public officers. Why should we suffer ourselves to be cheated by sounding names and fair shows? The titles, the property, the notoriety, the brief consequence of our fellows are only the decoration of the sacrifice, and add to the melancholy of the observer.

> "The earth goes on the earth glittering with gold,
> The earth goes to the earth sooner than it should,
> The earth builds on the earth castles and towers,
> The earth says to the earth, all this is ours."

All this is covered up by the speedy succession of the particulars, which tread so close on each other's heel, as to allow no space for the man to question the whole thing. There is somewhat terrific in this mask of routine. Captain Franklin, after six weeks travelling on the ice to the North Pole, found himself two hundred miles south of the spot he had set out from. The ice had floated; and we sometimes start to think we are spelling out the same sentences, saying the same words, repeating the same acts as in former years. Our ice may float also.

This preponderance of the senses can we balance and redress? Can we give permanence to the lightnings of thought which lick up in a moment these combustible mountains of sensation and custom, and reveal the moral order after which the world is to be rebuilt anew? Grave questions truly, but such as leave us no option. To know the facts is already a choosing of sides, ranges us on the party of Light and Reason, sounds the signal for the strife, and prophesies an end to the insanity and a restoration of the balance and rectitude of man.

TRANSCENDENTALISM

JANUARY, 1842

THE more liberal thought of intelligent persons acquires a new name in each period or community; and in ours, by no very good luck, as it sometimes appears to us, has been designated as Transcendentalism. We have every day occasion to remark its perfect identity, under whatever new phraseology or application to new facts, with the liberal thought of all men of a religious and contemplative habit in other times and countries. We were lately so much struck with two independent testimonies to this fact, proceeding from persons, one in sympathy with the Quakers, and the other with the Calvinistic Church, that we have begged the privilege to transcribe an extract from two private letters, in order that we might bring them together.

The Calvinist writes to his Correspondent after this manner.

" All the peculiarities of the theology, denominated Trinitarian, are directly or indirectly transcendental. The sinfulness of man involves the supposition of a nature in man, which transcends all limits of animal life and of social moralities. The reality of spirit, in the highest sense of that holy word, as the essence of God and the inward ground and law of man's being and doing, is supposed both in the fact of sin, and the possibility of redemption from sin. The mystery of the Father revealed only in the Son as the Word of Life, the Light which illumines every man, outwardly in the incarnation and offering for sin, inwardly as the Christ in us, energetic and quickening in the inspirations of the Holy Spirit, — the great mystery wherein we find redemption, this, like the rest, is transcendental. So throughout, as might be shown by the same induction suggested in relation to another aspect of the matter. Now here is my point. Trinitarians, whose whole system from beginning to end is transcendental, ideal, — an idea is the highest truth, — war against the very foundations of whatever is transcendental, ideal; all must be empiric, sensuous, inductive. A system, which used to create and sustain the most fervid enthusiasm, as is its nature, for it makes God all in all, leads in crusade against all even the purest and gentlest enthusiasm. It fights for the letter of Orthodoxy, for usage, for custom, for tradition, against the Spirit as it breathes like healing air through the damps and unwholesome swamps, or like strong wind throwing down rotten trees and rotten frameworks of men. It builds up with one hand the Temple of Truth on the outside; and with the other works as in frenzy to tear up its very foundations. So has it seemed to me. The transcendentalists do not err in excess but in defect, if I understand the case. They do not hold wild dreams for realities; the vision is deeper, broader, more spiritual than they have seen. They do not believe with too strong faith; their faith is too dim of sight, too feeble of grasp, too wanting in certainty. I regret that they should ever seem to undervalue the Scriptures. For those scriptures have flowed out of the same spirit which is in every pure heart; and I would have the one spirit recognize and respond to itself under all the multiform shapes of word, of deed, of faith, of love, of thought, of affection, in which it is enrobed; just as that spirit in us recognizes and responds to itself now in the gloom of winter, now in the cheer of summer, now in the bloom of spring, now in the maturity of autumn; and in all the endless varieties of each."

The Friend writes thus.

"Hold fast, I beseech you, to the resolution to wait for light from the Lord. Go not to men for a creed, faint not, but be of good courage. The darkness is only for a season. We must be willing to tarry the Lord's time in the wilderness, if we would enter the Promised Land. The purest saints that I have ever known were long, very long, in darkness and in doubt. Even when they had firm faith, they were long without *feeling* what they *believed in*. One told me he was two years in chaotic darkness, without an inch of firm ground to stand upon, watching for the day-spring from on high, and after this long probation it shone upon his path, and he has walked by its light for years. Do not fear or regret your isolation from men, your difference from all around you. It is often necessary to the enlargement of the soul that it should thus dwell alone for a season, and when the mystical union of God and man shall be completely developed, and you feel yourself newly born a child of light, one of the sons of God, you will also feel new ties to your fellow men; you will love them all in God, and each will be to you whatever their state will permit them to be.

"It is very interesting to me to see, as I do, all around me here, the essential doctrines of the Quakers revived, modified, stript of all that puritanism and sectarianism had heaped upon them, and made the foundation of an intellectual philosophy, that is illuminating the finest minds and reaches the wants of the least cultivated. The more I reflect upon the Quakers, the more I admire the early ones, and am surprised at their being so far in advance of their age, but they have educated the world till it is now able to go beyond those teachers.

"Spiritual growth, which they considered at variance with intellectual culture, is now wedded to it, and man's whole nature is advanced. The intellectual had so lorded it over the moral, that much onesided cultivation was requisite to make things even. I remember when your intellect was all in all, and the growth of the moral sense came after. It has now taken its proper place in your mind, and the intellect appears for a time prostrate, but in due season both will go on harmoniously, and you will be a perfect man. If you suffer more than many before coming into the light, it is because your character is deeper and your happy enlargement will be proportioned to it."

The identity, which the writer of this letter finds between the speculative opinions of serious persons at the present moment, and those entertained by the first Quakers, is indeed so striking as to have drawn a very general attention of late years to the history of that sect. . . . Of course, in proportion to the depth of the experience, will be its independence on time and circumstances, yet one can hardly read George Fox's Journal, or Sewel's History of the Quakers, without many a rising of joyful surprise at the correspondence of facts and expressions to states of thought and feeling, with which we are very familiar. The writer justly remarks the equal adaptation of the philosophy in question "to the finest minds, and to the least cultivated." And so we add in regard to these works, that quite apart from the pleasure of reading modern history in old books, the reader will find another reward in the abundant illustration they furnish to the fact, that wherever the religious enthusiasm makes its appearance, it supplies the place of poetry and philosophy and of learned discipline, and inspires by itself the same vastness of thinking; so that in learning the religious experiences of a strong but untaught mind, you seem to have suggested in turn all the sects of the philosophers.

We seize the occasion to adorn our pages with the dying speech of James Naylor, one of the companions of Fox, who had previously been for eight years a common soldier in the army. Its least service will be to show how far the religious sentiment could exalt the thinking and purify the language of the most uneducated men.

" There is a spirit which I feel," said James Naylor a few hours before his death, " that delights to do no evil, nor to revenge any wrong, but delights to endure all things, in hope to enjoy its own in the end. Its hope is to outlive all wrath and contention, and to weary out all exultation and cruelty, or whatever is of a nature contrary to itself. It sees to the end of all temptations. As it bears no evil in itself, so it conceives none in thought to any other. If it be betrayed, it bears it; for its ground and spring is the mercies and forgiveness of God. Its crown is meekness, its life is everlasting love unfeigned, and it takes its kingdom with entreaty, and keeps it by lowliness of mind. In God alone it can rejoice, though none else regard it, or can own its life. It is conceived in sorrow, and brought forth without any to pity it; nor doth it murmur at grief and oppression. It never rejoiceth but through sufferings; for with the world's joy it is murdered. I found it alone being forsaken. I have fellowship therein with them who lived in dens and desolate places of the earth, who through death obtained this resurrection and eternal holy life."

VEESHNOO SARMA

JULY, 1842

WE commence in the present number the printing of a series of selections from the oldest ethical and religous writings of men, exclusive of the Hebrew and Greek Scriptures. Each nation has its bible more or less pure; none has yet been willing or able in a wise and devout spirit to collate its own with those of other nations, and sinking the civil-historical and the ritual portions to bring together the grand expressions of the moral sentiment in different ages and races, the rules for the guidance of life, the bursts of piety and of abandonment to the Invisible and Eternal; — a work inevitable sooner or later, and which we hope is to be done by religion and not by literature.

The following sentences are taken from Charles Wilkins's translation of the Heetopades or Amicable Instructions of Veeshnoo Sarma, according to Sir William Jones, the most beautiful, if not the most ancient collection of apologues in the world, and the original source of the book, which passes in the modern languages of Europe and America, under the false name of Pilpay.

EXTRACTS FROM THE HEETOPADES OF VEESHNOO SARMA

Whatsoever cometh to pass, either good or evil, is the consequence of a man's own actions, and descendeth from the power of the Supreme Ruler.

Our lives are for the purposes of religion, labor, love, and salvation. If these are destroyed, what is not lost? If these are preserved, what is not preserved?

A wise man should relinquish both his wealth and his life for another. All is to be surrendered for a just man when he is reduced to the brink of destruction.

Why dost thou hesitate over this perishable body composed of flesh, bones, and excrements? O my friend, [*my body,*] support my reputation!

If constancy is to be obtained by inconstancy, purity by impurity, reputation by the body, then what is there which may not be obtained?

The difference between the body and the qualities is infinite; the body is a thing to be destroyed in a moment, whilst the qualities endure to the end of the creation.

Is this one of us, or is he a stranger? is the enumeration of the ungenerous; but to those by whom liberality is practised, the whole world is but as one family.

Fortune attendeth that lion amongst men who exerteth himself. They are weak men who declare Fate the sole cause.

It is said, Fate is nothing but the deeds committed in a former state of existence; wherefore it behoveth a man vigilantly to exert the powers he is possessed of.

The stranger, who turneth away from a house with disappointed hopes, leaveth there his own offences and departeth, taking with him all the good actions of the owner.

Hospitality is to be exercised even towards an enemy when he cometh to thine house. The tree does not withdraw its shade even from the wood-cutter.

Of all men thy guest is the superior.

The mind of a good man does not alter when he is in distress; the waters of the ocean are not to be heated by a torch of straw.

Nor bathing with cool water, nor a necklace of pearls, nor anointing with sanders, yieldeth such comfort to the body oppressed with heat, as the language of a good man cheerfully uttered doth to the mind.

Good men extend their pity even unto the most despicable animals. The moon doth not withhold the light, even from the cottage of a Chandala.

Those who have forsaken the killing of all; those who are helpmates to all; those who are a sanctuary to all; those men are in the way to heaven.

Behold the difference between the one who eateth flesh, and him to whom it belonged. The first hath a momentary enjoyment, whilst the latter is deprived of existence.

Who would commit so great a crime against a poor animal, who is fed only by the herbs which grow wild in the woods, and whose belly is burnt up with hunger?

Every book of knowledge, which is known to Oosana or to Vreehaspatee, is by nature planted in the understanding of women.

The beauty of the Kokeela is his voice; the beauty of a wife is constancy to her husband; the beauty of the ill-favored is science; the beauty of the penitent is patience.

What is too great a load for those who have strength? What is distance to the indefatigable? What is a foreign country to those who have science? Who is a stranger to those who have the habit of speaking kindly?

Time drinketh up the essence of every great and noble action, which ought to be performed and is delayed in the execution.

When Nature is forsaken by her lord, be she ever so great, she doth not survive.

Suppose thyself a river, and a holy pilgrimage in the land of Bharata, of which truth is the water, good actions the banks, and compassion the current; and then, O son of Pandoo, wash thyself therein, for the inward soul is not to be purified by common water.

As frogs to the pool, as birds to a lake full of water, so doth every species of wealth flow to the hands of him who exerteth himself.

If we are rich with the riches which we neither give nor enjoy, we are rich with the riches which are buried in the caverns of the earth.

He whose mind is at ease is possessed of all riches. Is it not the same to one whose foot is enclosed in a shoe, as if the whole surface of the earth were covered with leather?

Where have they, who are running here and there in search of riches, such happiness as those placid spirits enjoy who are gratified at the immortal fountain of happiness?

All hath been read, all hath been heard, and all hath been followed by him who, having put hope behind him, dependeth not upon expectation.

What is religion? Compassion for all things which have life. What is happiness? To animals in this world, health. What is kindness? A principle in the good. What is philosophy? An entire separation from the world.

To a hero of sound mind, what is his own, and what a foreign country? Wherever he halteth, that place is acquired by the splendor of his arms.

When pleasure is arrived, it is worthy of attention; when trouble presenteth itself, the same; pains and pleasures have their revolutions like a wheel.

One, although not possessed of a mine of gold, may find the offspring of his own nature, that noble ardor which hath for its object the accomplishment of the whole assemblage of virtues.

Man should not be over-anxious for a subsistence, for it is provided by the Creator. The infant no sooner droppeth from the womb, than the breasts of the mother begin to stream.

He, by whom geese were made white, parrots are stained green, and peacocks painted of various hues, — even he will provide for their support.

He, whose inclination turneth away from an object, may be said to have obtained it.

FOURIERISM AND THE SOCIALISTS

JULY, 1842

THE increasing zeal and numbers of the disciples of Fourier, in America and in Europe, entitle them to an attention which their theory and practical projects will justify and reward. In London, a good weekly newspaper (lately changed into a monthly journal) called " The Phalanx," devoted to the social doctrines of Charles Fourier, and bearing for its motto, " Association and Colonization," is edited by Hugh Doherty. Mr. Etzler's inventions, as described in the Phalanx, promise to cultivate twenty thousand acres with the aid of four men only and cheap machinery. Thus the laborers are threatened with starvation, if they do not organize themselves into corporations, so that machinery may labor *for* instead of working *against* them. It appears that Mr. Young, an Englishman of large property, has purchased the Benedictine Abbey of Citeaux, in the Mont d'Or, in France, with its ample domains, for the purpose of establishing a colony there. We also learn that some members of the sect have bought an estate at Santa Catharina, fifty miles from Rio Janeiro, in a good situation for an agricultural experiment, and one hundred laborers have sailed from Havre to that port, and nineteen hundred more are to follow. On the anniversary of the birthday of Fourier, which occurred in April, public festivals were kept by the Socialists in London, in Paris, and in New York. In the city of New York, the disciples of Fourier have bought a column in the Daily Tribune, Horace Greeley's excellent newspaper, whose daily and weekly circulation exceeds twenty thousand copies, and through that organ are now diffusing their opinions.

We had lately an opportunity of learning something of these Socialists and their theory from the indefatigable apostle of the sect in New York, Albert Brisbane. Mr. Brisbane pushes his doctrine with all the force of memory, talent, honest faith, and importunacy. As we listened to his exposition, it appeared to us the sublime of mechanical philosophy; for the system was the perfection of arrangement and contrivance. The force of arrangement could no farther go. The merit of the plan was that it was a system; that it had not the partiality and hint-and-fragment character of most popular schemes, but was coherent and comprehensive of facts to a wonderful degree. It was not daunted by distance, or magnitude, or remoteness of any sort, but strode about nature with a giant's step, and skipped no fact, but wove its large Ptolemaic web of cycle and epicycle, of phalanx and phalanstery, with laudable assiduity. Mechanics were pushed so far as fairly to meet spiritualism. One could not but be struck with strange coincidences betwixt Fourier and Swedenborg. Genius hitherto has been shamefully misapplied, a mere trifler. It must now set itself to raise the social condition of man, and to redress the disorders of the planet he inhabits. The Desert of Sahara, the Campagna di Roma, the frozen polar circles, which by their pestilential or hot or cold airs poison the temperate regions, accuse man. Society, concert, co-operation, is the secret of the coming Paradise. By reason of the isolation of men at the present day, all work is drudgery. By concert, and the allowing each laborer to choose his own work, it becomes pleasure. "Attractive Industry" would speedily subdue, by adventurous, scientific, and persistent tillage, the pestilential tracts; would equalize temperature; give health to the globe, and cause the earth to yield "healthy imponderable fluids" to the solar system, as now it yields noxious fluids. The hyæna, the jackal, the gnat, the bug, the flea, were all beneficent parts of the system; the good Fourier knew what those creatures should have been, had not the mould slipped, through the bad state of the atmosphere, caused, no doubt, by these same vicious imponderable fluids. All these shall be redressed by human culture, and the useful goat, and dog, and innocent poetical moth, or the wood-tick to consume decomposing wood, shall take their place. It takes 1680 men to make one Man, complete in all the faculties; that is, to be sure that you have got a good joiner, a good cook, a barber, a poet, a judge, an umbrella-maker, a mayor and aldermen, and so on. Your community should consist of 2000 persons, to prevent accidents of omission; and each community should take up 6000 acres of land. Now fancy the earth planted with fifties and hundreds of these phalanxes side by side, — what tillage, what architecture, what refectories, what dormitories, what reading rooms, what concerts, what lectures, what gardens, what baths! What is not in one, will be in another, and many will be within easy distance. Then know you and all, that Constantinople is the natural capital of the globe. There, in the Golden Horn, will be the Arch-Phalanx established, there will the Omniarch reside. Aladdin and his magician, or the beautiful Scheherzarade, can alone in these prosaic times, before the sight, describe the material splendors collected there. Poverty shall be abolished; deformity, stupidity, and crime shall be no more. Genius, grace, art, shall abound, and it is not to be doubted but that, in the reign of "Attractive Industry," all men will speak in blank verse.

Certainly we listened with great pleasure to such gay and magnificent pictures. The ability and earnestness of the advocate and his friends, the comprehensiveness of their theory, its apparent directness of proceeding to the end they would secure, the indignation they felt and uttered at all other speculation in the presence of so much social misery, commanded our attention and respect. It contained so much truth, and promised in the attempts that shall be made to realize it so much valuable instruction, that we are engaged to observe every step of its progress. Yet in spite of the assurances of its friends, that it was new and widely discriminated from all other plans for the regeneration of society we could not exempt it from the criticism which we apply to so many projects for reform with which the brain of the age teems. Our feeling was, that Fourier had skipped no fact but one, namely, Life. He treats man as a plastic thing, something that may be put up or down, ripened or retarded, moulded, polished, made into solid, or fluid, or gas, at the will of the leader; or, perhaps, as a vegetable, from which, though now a poor crab, a very good peach can by manure and exposure be in time produced, but skips the faculty of life, which spawns and scorns system and system-makers, which eludes all conditions, which makes or supplants a thousand phalanxes and New-Harmonies with each pulsation. There is an order in which in a sound mind the faculties always appear, and which, according to the strength of the individual, they seek to realize in the surrounding world. The value of Fourier's system is that it is a statement of such an order externized, or carried outward into its correspondence in facts. The mistake is, that this particular order and series is to be imposed by force of preaching and votes on all men, and carried into rigid execution. But what is true and good must not only be begun by life, but must be conducted to its issues by life. Could not the conceiver of this design have also believed that a similar model lay in every mind, and that the method of each associate might be trusted, as well as that of his particular Committee and General Office, No. 200 Broadway? nay, that it would be better to say, let us be lovers and servants of that which is just; and straightaway every man becomes a centre of a holy and beneficent republic, which he sees to include all men in its law, like that of Plato, and of Christ. Before such a man the whole world becomes Fourierized or Christized or humanized, and in the obedience to his most private being, he finds himself, according to his presentiment, though against all sensuous probability, acting in strict concert with all others who followed their private light.

Yet in a day of small, sour, and fierce schemes, one is admonished and cheered by a project of such friendly aims, and of such bold and generous proportion; there is an intellectual courage and strength in it, which is superior and commanding: it certifies the presence of so much truth in the theory, and in so far is destined to be fact.

But now, whilst we write these sentences, comes to us a paper from Mr. Brisbane himself. We are glad of the opportunity of letting him speak for himself. He has much more to say than we have hinted, and here has treated a general topic. We have not room for quite all the matter which he has sent us, but persuade ourselves that we have retained every material statement, in spite of the omissions which we find it necessary to make, to contract his paper to so much room as we offered him.

Mr. Brisbane, in a prefatory note to his article, announces himself as an advocate of the Social Laws discovered by Charles Fourier, and intimates that he wishes to connect whatever value attaches to any statement of his, with the work in which he is exclusively engaged, that of Social Reform. He adds the following broad and generous declaration.

"It seems to me that, with the spectacle of the present misery and degradation of the human race before us, all scientific researches and speculations, to be of any real value, should have a bearing upon the means of their social elevation and happiness. The mass of scientific speculations, which are every day offered to the world by men, who are not animated by a deep interest in the elevation of their race, and who exercise their talents merely to build up systems, or to satisfy a spirit of controversy, or personal ambition, are perfectly valueless. What is more futile than barren philosophical speculation, that leads to no great practical results?"

INTELLIGENCE

JULY, 1842

Exploring Expedition. The United States Corvette Vincennes, Captain Charles Wilkes, the flag ship of the Exploring Expedition, arrived at New York on Friday, June 10th, from a cruise of nearly four years. The Brigs Porpoise and Oregon may shortly be expected. The Expedition has executed every part of the duties confided to it by the Government. A long list of ports, harbors, islands, reefs, and shoals, named in the list, have been visited and examined or surveyed. The positions assigned on the charts to several vigias, reefs, shoals, and islands, have been carefully looked for, run over, and found to have no existence in or near the places assigned them. Several of the principal groups and islands in the Pacific Ocean have been visited, examined, and surveyed; and friendly intercourse, and protective commercial regulations, established with the chiefs and natives. The discoveries in the Antarctic Ocean (Antarctic continent, — observations for fixing the Southern Magnetic pole, &c.) *preceded* those of the French and English expeditions. The Expedition, during its absence, has also examined and surveyed a large portion of the Oregon Territory, a part of Upper California, including the Columbia and Sacramento Rivers, with their various tributaries. Several exploring parties from the Squadron have explored, examined, and fixed those portions of the Oregon Territory least known. A map of the Territory, embracing its Rivers, Sounds, Harbors, Coasts, Forts, &c., has been prepared, which will furnish the information relative to our possessions on the Northwest Coast, and the whole of Oregon. Experiments have been made with the pendulum, magnetic apparatus, and various other instruments, on all occasions, — the temperature of the ocean, at various depths, ascertained in the different seas traversed, and full meteorological and other observations kept up during the cruise. Charts of all the surveys have been made, with views and sketches of headlands, towns or villages, &c., with descriptions of all that appertains to the localities, productions, language, customs, and manners. At some of the islands, this duty has been attended with much labor, exposure, and risk of life, — the treacherous character of the natives rendering it absolutely necessary that the officers and men should be armed, while on duty, and at all times prepared against their murderous attacks. On several occasions, boats have been absent from the different vessels of the Squadron on surveying duty, (the greater part of which has been performed in boats,) among islands, reefs, &c., for a period of ten, twenty, and thirty days at one time. On one of these occasions, two of the officers were killed at the Fiji group, while defending their boat's crew from an attack by the Natives.

Association of State Geologists. After holding annual meetings in New York and Philadelphia, the Geologists assembled in April of this year in Boston, to the number of forty, from the most distant points of the Union. Members were present from Natchez and Iowa. Mr. Lyell from London was present. From we know not what inadvertence, the notice of so unusual a scientific union failed to reach the ancient ears of the University, at three miles' distance.

Neither its head nor its members, neither the professor of Geology nor the professor of Physics arrived to welcome these pilgrims of science, from the far East and the far West, to the capital and University of New England. The public Address was made by Mr. Silliman, and reports and debates of the most animated and various interest, by the Messrs. Rogers of Pennsylvania and of Virginia, Dr. Morton of Philadelphia, and others, a full report of which is in the course of publication. The next annual meeting is to be holden in Albany, N. Y.

Harvard University. The Chair of Natural History, vacant since the resignation of Mr. Nuttall, is filled by the appointment of Asa Gray, M. D., known to the botanists as the associate of Mr. Torrey of New York. In the Divinity College, the Chair of Pulpit Eloquence and Pastoral Care, vacant by the resignation of Henry Ware, Jr., is to be filled by Dr. Convers Francis. A generous subscription by several friends of the College has resulted in a fund of more than 20,000 dollars for the purchase of books for the College Library. The College has also received a bequest which promises at a future day to be a valuable foundation. Benjamin Bussey, Esq. has provided in his will for the application of the income of his property to the benefit of certain heirs therein named. At the decease of the survivor of them, and subject to the payment of any annuities then existing, he gives all his property to Harvard University for the following purposes. His Estate in Roxbury is to be held forever as a Seminary for "instruction in practical agriculture, in useful and ornamental gardening, in botany, and in such other branches of natural science, as may tend to promote a knowledge of practical agriculture, and the various arts subservient thereto, and connected therewith." The government of the University is also "to cause such courses of lectures to be delivered there, at such seasons of the year and under such regulations as they may think best adapted to promote the ends designed; and also to furnish gratuitous aid, if they shall think it expedient, to such meritorious persons as may resort there for instruction." One half of the net income of his property is to be appropriated to maintain that institution; and the residue of the income is to be divided equally between the Divinity School and the Law School of the University. Mr. Bussey's property is estimated at not less than three hundred and fifty thousand dollars.

On the subject of the University we cannot help wishing that a change will one day be adopted which will put an end to the foolish bickering between the government and the students, which almost every year breaks out into those uncomfortable fracases which are called "Rebellions." Cambridge is so well endowed, and offers such large means of education, that it can easily assume the position of an University, and leave to the numerous younger Colleges the charge of pupils too young to be trusted from home. This is instantly effected by the Faculty's confining itself to the office of Instruction, and omitting to assume the office of Parietal Government. Let the College provide the best teachers in each department, and for a stipulated price receive the pupil to its lecture-rooms and libraries; but in the matter of morals and manners, leave the student to his own conscience, and if he is a bad subject to the ordinary police. This course would have the effect of keeping back pupils from College, a year or two, or, in some cases, of bringing the parents or guardians of the pupil to reside in Cambridge; but it would instantly destroy the root of endless grievances between the student and teacher, put both parties on the best footing, — indispensable, one would say, to good teaching, — and relieve the professors of an odious guardianship, always degenerating into espionage, which must naturally indispose men of genius and honorable mind from accepting the professor's chair.

From London we have Mr. Wordsworth's new volume of poems, which is not a bookseller's book, but a poet's book. We have read them all with great content, and very willingly forgave the poet for writing against the abolition of capital punishment, for the sake of the self-respect and truth to his own character, which the topic and the treatment evinced. We should say the same thing of his sonnet levelled at Mr. Thomas Carlyle. But the name of Wordsworth reminds us of another matter far less pleasant than poetry, namely, the profligate course recently adopted by some of the States of the Union in relation to their public debt. The following is an extract from a letter of Mr. Wordsworth to Bishop Doane of New Jersey. "The proceedings of some of the States in your country, in money concerns, and the shock which is given to the credit of the State of Pennsylvania, have caused much trouble under our roof, by the injury done to some of my most valuable connexions and friends. I am not personally and directly a sufferer; but my brother, if the State of Pennsylvania should fail to fulfil its engagements, would lose almost all the little savings of his long and generous life. My daughter, through the perfidy of the State of Mississippi, has forfeited a sum, though but small in itself, large for her means; a great portion of my most valued friends have to lament their misplaced confidence. Topics of this kind are not pleasant to dwell upon, but the more extensively the injury is made known, the more likely is it, that where any remains of integrity, honor, or even common humanity exist, efforts will be made to set and keep things right." We have learned also with mortification that John Sterling, whose poems have been lately reprinted in this country, had invested £2000 in the worthless stock of the Morris Canal Company, and later, that Mr. Carlyle had invested $1000 in stock of the State of Illinois, which presently proved worthless. In this way the heavens have taken care that the character of our rotten public stocks and the doctrine of "Repudiation" shall be damned to fame.

Alfred Tennyson, moved by being informed of his American popularity, has given himself to the labor of revising and reprinting a selection of his old poems, and adding as many new ones, which he has sent to Mr. Wheeler of Harvard University, who is republishing them here.

Henry Taylor, too, the author of Van Artevelde, announces a new dramatic poem in press in London. John Sterling is still engaged on a tragedy, "Strafford," which should have been finished before this time, but for the ill health of the poet, which has driven him to the south of Italy. Thomas Carlyle is understood to be engaged on the Life of Oliver Cromwell.

Berlin. From Berlin, "The City of Criticism," we learned, in the past months, that the king of Prussia was gathering around him a constellation of men of science. The city was already the residence of Humboldt, of Bettine von Arnim, of Raumer, of Ranke, of Ritter, and of Ehrenberg. G. F. Waagen is director of the Royal Gallery; and now Cornelius, the great fresco painter; Ruckert, the poet; Tholuck, the theologian; and, greatest of all, Schelling, from Munich, are there. The king is discontented with the Hegel influence, which has predominated at Berlin, and, we regret to say, set himself to suppress the "Hallische Jahrbucher;" which, though published at Halle, depended for its support mainly on Berlin. With this view, also, he summons the great Schelling, now nearly seventy years old, to lecture on the Philosophy of Revelation. We have private accounts of this lectures, which began in the last November. The lecture room was crowded to suffocation; the pale professor, whose face resembles that of Socrates, was greeted with thunders of acclamation, but he remained pale and unmoved as if in his own study, and apparently quite unconscious that he was making a new epoch in German history. His first lecture has been published at Berlin. Such are the social and æsthetic attractions of this city, that it is said to acquire a new population of six thousand souls every year, by the residence of travellers, who are arrested by its music, its theatre, and the arts.

ENGLISH REFORMERS

OCTOBER, 1842

WHILST Mr. Sparks visits England to explore the manuscripts of the Colonial Office, and Dr. Waagen on a mission of Art, Mr. Alcott, whose genius and efforts in the great art of Education have been more appreciated in England than in America, has now been spending some months in that country, with the aim to confer with the most eminent Educators and philanthropists, in the hope to exchange intelligence, and import into this country whatever hints have been struck out there, on the subject of literature and the First Philosophy. The design was worthy, and its first results have already reached us. Mr. Alcott was received with great cordiality of joy and respect by his friends in London, and presently found himself domesticated at an institution, managed on his own methods and called after his name, the School of Mr. Wright at Alcott House, Ham, Surrey. He was introduced to many men of literary and philanthropic distinction, and his arrival was made the occasion of meetings for public conversation on the great ethical questions of the day.

Mr. Alcott's mission, beside making us acquainted with the character and labors of some excellent persons, has loaded our table with a pile of English books, pamphlets, periodicals, flying prospectuses, and advertisements, proceeding from a class very little known in this country, and on many accounts important, the party, namely, who represent Social Reform. Here are Educational Circulars, and Communist Apostles; Alists; Plans for Syncretic Associations, and Pestalozzian Societies, Self-supporting Institutions, Experimental Normal Schools, Hydropathic and Philosophical Associations, Health Unions and Phalansterian Gazettes, Paradises within the reach of all men, Appeals of Man to Woman, and Necessities of Internal Marriage illustrated by Phrenological Diagrams. These papers have many sins to answer for. There is an abundance of superficialness, of pedantry, of inflation, and of want of thought. It seems as if these sanguine schemers rushed to the press with every notion that danced before their brain, and clothed it in the most clumsily compounded and terminated words, for want of time to find the right one. But although these men sometimes use a swollen and vicious diction, yet they write to ends which raise them out of the jurisdiction of ordinary criticism. They speak to the conscience, and have that superiority over the crowd of their contemporaries, which belongs to men who entertain a good hope. Moreover, these pamphlets may well engage the attention of the politician, as straws of no mean significance to show the tendencies of the time.

Mr. Alcott's visit has brought us nearer to a class of Englishmen, with whom we had already some slight but friendly correspondence, who possess points of so much attraction for us, that we shall proceed to give a short account both of what we already knew, and what we have lately learned, concerning them. The central figure in the group is a very remarkable person, who for many years, though living in great retirement, has made himself felt by many of the best and ablest men in England and in Europe, we mean James Pierrepont Greaves, who died at Alcott-

House in the month of March of this year. Mr. Greaves was formerly a wealthy merchant in the city of London, but was deprived of his property by French spoliations in Napoleon's time. Quitting business, he travelled and resided for some time in Germany. His leisure was given to books of the deepest character; and in Switzerland he found a brother in Pestalozzi. With him he remained ten years, living abstemiously, almost on biscuit and water; and though they never learned each the other's language, their daily intercourse appears to have been of the deepest and happiest kind. Mr. Greaves there made himself useful in a variety of ways. Pestalozzi declared that Mr. Greaves understood his aim and methods better than any other observer. And he there became acquainted with some eminent persons. Mr. Greaves on his return to England introduced as much as he could of the method and life, whose beautiful and successful operations he had witnessed; and although almost all that he did was misunderstood, or dragged downwards, he has been a chief instrument in the regeneration in the British schools. For a single and unknown individual his influence has been extensive. He set on foot Infant Schools, and was for many years Secretary to the Infant School Society, which office brought him in contact with many parties, and he has connected himself with almost every effort for human emancipation. In this work he was engaged up to the time of his death. His long and active career developed his own faculties and powers in a wonderful manner. At his house, No. 49 Burton Street, London, he was surrounded by men of open and accomplished minds, and his doors were thrown open weekly for meetings for the discussion of universal subjects. In the last years he has resided at Cheltenham, and visited Stockport for the sake of acquainting himself with the Socialists and their methods.

His active and happy career continued nearly to the seventieth year, with heart and head unimpaired and undaunted, his eyes and other faculties sound, except his lower limbs, which suffered from his sedentary occupation of writing. For nearly thirty-six years he abstained from all fermented drinks, and all animal food. In the last years he dieted almost wholly on fruit. The private correspondent, from whose account, written two years ago, we have derived our sketch, proceeds in these words. " Through evil reports, revilings, seductions, and temptations many and severe, the Spirit has not let him go, but has strongly and securely held him, in a manner not often witnessed. New consciousness opens to him every day. His literary abilities would not be by critics entitled to praise, nor does he speak with what is called eloquence; but as he is so much the 'lived word,' I have described, there is found a potency in all he writes and all he says, which belongs not to beings less devoted to the Spirit. Supplies of money have come to him as fast, or nearly as fast as required, and at all events his serenity was never disturbed on this account, unless when it has happened that, having more than his expenses required, he has volunteered extraneous expenditures. He has been, I consider, a great apostle of the Newness to many, even when neither he nor they knew very clearly what was going forward. Thus inwardly married, he has remained outwardly a bachelor."

Mr. Greaves is described to us by another correspondent as being " the soul of his circle, a prophet of whom the world heard nothing, but who has quickened much of the thought now current in the most intellectual circles of the kingdom. He was acquainted with every man of deep character in England, and many both in Germany and Switzerland; and Strauss, the author of the 'Life of Christ,' was a pupil of Mr. Greaves, when he held conversations in one of the Colleges of Germany, after leaving Pestalozzi. A most remarkable man; nobody remained the same after leaving him. He was the prophet of the deepest affirmative truths, and no man ever sounded his depths. The best of the thought in the London Monthly Magazine was the transcript of his Idea. He read and wrote much, chiefly in the manner of Coleridge, with pen in hand, in the form of notes on the text of his author. But, like Boehmen and Swedenborg, neither his thoughts nor his writings were for the popular mind. His favorites were the chosen illuminated minds of all time, and with them he was familiar. His library is the most select and rare which I have seen, including most of the books which we have sought with so ill success on our side of the water."[1]

His favorite dogma was the superiority of Being to

[1] The following notice of Mr. Greaves occurs in Mr. Morgan's "Hampden in the Nineteenth Century." "The gentleman whom he met at the school was Mr. J. P. Greaves, at that time Honorary Secretary to the Infant School Society, and a most active and disinterested promoter of the system. He had resided for three(?) years with Pestalozzi, who set greater value upon right feelings and rectitude of conduct, than upon the acquisition of languages. A collection of highly interesting letters, addressed to this gentleman by Pestalozzi on the subject of education, has been published. Among the numerous advocates for various improvements, there was not one who exceeded him in personal sacrifices to what he esteemed a duty. At the same time he had some peculiar opinions, resembling the German mystical and metaphysical speculations, hard to be understood, and to which few in general are willing to listen, and still fewer to subscribe; but his sincerity, and the kindness of his disposition always secured for him a patient hearing." — Vol. II. p. 22.

all knowing and doing. Association on a high basis was his ideal for the present conjuncture. "I hear every one crying out for association," said he; "I join in the cry; but then I say, associate first with the Spirit, — educate for this spirit-association; and far more will follow than we have as yet any idea of. Nothing good can be done without association; but then we must associate with goodness; and this goodness is the spirit-nature, without which all our societarian efforts will be turned to corruption. Education has hitherto been all outward; it must now be inward. The educator must keep in view that which elevates man, and not the visible exterior world." We have the promise of some extracts from the writings of this great man, which we hope shortly to offer to the readers of this Journal. His friend, Mr. Lane, is engaged in arranging and editing his manuscript remains.

Mr. Heraud, a poet and journalist, chiefly known in this country as the editor for two years of the (London) Monthly Magazine, a disciple, in earlier years, of Coleridge, and by nature and taste contemplative and inclined to a mystical philosophy, was a friend and associate of Mr. Greaves; and for the last years has been more conspicuous than any other writer in that connexion of opinion. The Monthly Magazine, during his editorship, really was conducted in a bolder and more creative spirit than any other British Journal; and though papers on the highest transcendental themes were found in odd vicinity with the lowest class of flash and so-called comic tales, yet a necessity, we suppose, of British taste made these strange bed-fellows acquainted, and Mr. Heraud had done what he could. His papers called "Foreign Aids to Self Intelligence," were of signal merit, especially the papers on Boehmen and Swedenborg. The last is, we think, the very first adequate attempt to do justice to this mystic, by an analysis of his total works; and, though avowedly imperfect, is, as far as it goes, a faithful piece of criticism. We hope that Mr. Heraud, who announces a work in three volumes, called "Foreign Aids to Self Intelligence, designed for an Historical Introduction to the Study of Ontological Science, preparatory to a Critique of Pure Being," as now in preparation for the press, and of which, we understand, the Essays in the Monthly Magazine were a part, will be enabled to fulfil his design. Mr. Heraud is described by his friends as the most amiable of men, and a fluent and popular lecturer on the affirmative philosophy. He has recently intimated a wish to cross the Atlantic, and read in Boston a course of six lectures, on the subject of Christism as distinct from Christianity.

One of the best contributors to Mr. Heraud's Magazine was Mr. J. Westland Marston. The papers marked with his initials are the most eloquent in the book. We have greatly regretted their discontinuance, and have hailed him again in his new appearance as a dramatic author. Mr. Marston is a writer of singular purity of taste, with a heart very open to the moral impulses, and in his settled conviction, like all persons of a high poetic nature, the friend of a universal reform, beginning in education. His thought on that subject is, that "it is only by teachers becoming men of genius, that a nobler position can be secured to them." At the same time he seems to share that disgust, which men of fine taste so quickly entertain in regard to the language and methods of that class with which their theory throws them into correspondence, and to be continually attracted through his taste to the manners and persons of the aristocracy, whose selfishness and frivolity displease and repel him again. Mr. Marston has lately written a Tragedy, called "The Patrician's Daughter," which we have read with great pleasure, barring always the fatal prescription, which in England seems to mislead every fine poet to attempt the drama. It must be the reading of tragedies that fills them with this superstition for the buskin and the pall, and not a sympathy with existing nature and the spirit of the age. The Patrician's Daughter is modern in its plot and characters; perfectly simple in its style; the dialogue is full of spirit, and the story extremely well told. We confess, as we drew out this bright pamphlet from amid the heap of crude declamation on Marriage and Education, on Dietetics and Hydropathy, on Chartism and Socialism, grim tracts on flesh-eating and dram-drinking, we felt the glad refreshment of its sense and melody, and thanked the fine office which speaks to the imagination, and paints with electric pencil a new form, — new forms on the lurid cloud. Although the vengeance of Mordaunt strikes us as overstrained, yet his character, and the growth of his fortunes is very natural, and is familiar to English experience, in the Thurlows, Burkes, Foxes, and Cannings. The Lady Mabel is finely drawn. Pity that the catastrophe should be wrought by the deliberate lie of Lady Lydia; for beside that lovers, as they of all men speak the most direct speech, easily pierce the cobwebs of fraud, it is a weak way of making a play, to hinge the crisis on a lie, instead of letting it grow, as in life, out of the faults and conditions of the parties, as, for example, in Goethe's Tasso. On all accounts but one, namely, the lapse of five years between two acts, the play seems to be eminently fit for representation. Mr. Marston is also the author of two tracts on Poetry and Poetic Culture.

Another member of this circle is Francis Barham,

the dramatic poet, author of "The Death of Socrates," a tragedy, and other pieces; also a contributor to the Monthly Magazine. To this gentleman we are under special obligations, as he has sent us, with other pamphlets, a manuscript paper "On American Literature," written with such flowing good will, and with an aim so high, that we must submit some portion of it to our readers.

"Intensely sympathizing, as I have ever done, with the great community of truth-seekers, I glory in the rapid progress of that Alistic,[1] or divine literature, which they develop and cultivate. To me this Alistic literature is so catholic and universal that it has spread its energies and influences through every age and na-

[1] In explanation of this term, we quote a few sentences from a printed prospectus issued by Mr. Barham. "*The Alist; a Monthly Magazine of Divinity and Universal Literature.* I have adopted the title of 'the Alist, or Divine,' for this periodical, because the extension of Divinity and divine truth is its main object. It appears to me, that by a firm adherence to the **το θειον**, or divine principle of things, a Magazine may assume a specific character, far more elevated, catholic, and attractive, than the majority of periodicals attain. This Magazine is therefore specially written for those persons who may, without impropriety, be termed Alists, or Divines; those who endeavor to develop Divinity as the grand primary essence of all existence, — the element which forms the all in all, — the element in which we live, and move, and have our being. Such Alists, (deriving their name from Alah — the Hebrew title of God,) are Divines in the highest sense of the word; for they cultivate Alism, or the Divinity of Divinities, as exhibited in all Scripture and nature, and they extend religious and philanthropical influences through all churches, states, and systems of education. This doctrine of Alism, or the life of God in the soul of man, affords the only prothetic point of union, sufficiently intense and authoritative to unite men in absolute catholicity. In proportion as they cultivate one and the same God in their minds, will their minds necessarily unite and harmonize; but without this is done, permanent harmony is impossible."

tion, in brighter or obscurer manifestations. It forms the intellectual patrimony of the universe, delivered down from kindling sire to kindling son, through all nations, peoples, and languages. Like the God from whom it springs, on whom it lives, and to whom it returns, this divine literature is ever young, ever old, ever present, ever remote. Like heaven's own sunshine, it adorns all it touches, and it touches all. It is a perfect cosmopolite in essence and in action; it has nothing local or limitary in its nature; it participates the character of the soul from which it emanated. It subsists whole in itself, it is its own place, its own time, nor seeks abroad the life it grants at home; aye, it is an eternal now, an eternal present, at once beginning, middle, and end of every past and every future.

" It is, I conceive, salutary for us to take this enlarged view of literature. We should seek after literary perfection in this cosmopolite spirit, and embrace it wherever we find it, as a divine gift; for, in the words of Pope,

> " 'both precepts and example tell
> That nature's masterpiece is writing well.'

" So was it with the august and prophetic Milton. To him literature was a universal presence. He regarded it as the common delight and glory of gods and men. He felt that its *moral beauty* lived and flourished in the large heart of humanity itself, and could never be monopolized by times or places. Most deeply do I think and feel with Milton, when he utters the following words. 'What God may have determined for me, I know not; but this I know, that if ever he instilled an intense love of moral beauty into the breast of any man, he has instilled it into mine. Hence wherever I find a man despising the false estimates of the vulgar, and daring to aspire in sentiment and language and conduct to what the highest wisdom through every age has taught us, as most excellent, to him I unite myself by a kind of necessary attachment. And if I am so influenced by nature, or destiny, that by no exertions or labors of my own I may exalt myself to this summit of worth and honor, yet no power in heaven or earth will hinder me from looking with reverence and affection upon those, who have thoroughly attained this glory, or appeared engaged in the successful pursuit of it.' "

Mr. Barham proceeds to apply this sentiment as analogous to his own sentiment, in respect to the literatures of other nations, but specially to that of America.

" The unity of language unites the literature of Britain and America, in an essential and imperishable marriage, which no Atlantic Ocean can divide. Yes; I as an Englishman say this, and maintain it. United in language, in literature, in interest, and in blood, I regard the English in England and the English in America as one and the same people, the same magnificent brotherhood. The fact is owned in the common names by which they are noted; John and Jonathan, Angles and Yankees, all reëcho the fact."

Mr. Barham proceeds to exhibit the manifold reasons that enjoin union on the two countries, deprecates the divisions that have sometimes suspended the peace, and continues:

" Let us rather maintain the generous policy of Milton, and with full acclamation of concord recite his inspiring words:

" ' Go on both hand in hand, O nations, never to be disunited. Be the praise and the heroic song of all posterity. Merit this, but seek only virtue, not the extension of your limits. For what needs to win a fading triumphal laurel out of the tears of wretched men, but to settle the true worship of God and justice in the commonwealth. Then shall the hardest difficulties smooth themselves out before you, envy shall sink to hell, and craft and malice shall be confounded, whether it be homebred mischief or outlandish cunning. Yea, other nations will then covet to serve you; for lordship and victory are but the pages of justice and virtue. Commit securely to true wisdom the vanquishing and uncaging of craft and subtlety, which are but her two runagates. Join your invincible might to do worthy and godlike deeds, and then he that seeks to break your union, a cleaving curse be his inheritance throughout all generations.' "

Mr. Barham then proceeds to express his conviction, that the specific character, which the literature of these countries should aim at, is the Alistic or Divine. It is only by an aim so high, that an author can reach any excellence.

> " He builds too low who builds beneath the skies."

But our limits forbid any more extracts from this friendly manuscript at present.

Another eminent member of this circle is Mr. Charles Lane, for many years manager of the London Mercantile Price Current; a man of a fine intellectual nature, inspired and hallowed by a profounder faith. Mr. Lane is the author of some pieces marked with his initials, in the Monthly Magazine, and of some remarkable tracts. Those which we have seen are, " The Old, the New-Old, and the New; " " Tone in Speech; " some papers in a Journal of Health; and last and best, a piece called " The Third Dispensation," prefixed by way of preface to an English translation of Mme. Gatti de Gamond's " Phalansterian," a French book of the Fourier School. In this Essay Mr. Lane considers that History has exhibited two dispensations, namely, *first,* the Family Union, or connexion by tribes, which soon appeared to be a disunion or a dispersive principle; *second,* the National Union. Both these, though better than the barbarism which they displaced, are themselves barbarism, in contrast with the *third,* or Universal Union.

"As man is the uniter in all arrangements which stand *below* him, and in which the objects could not unite themselves, so man needs a uniter *above* him, to whom he submits, in the certain incapability of self-union. This uniter, unity, or One, is the premonitor whence exists the premonition Unity, which so recurrently becomes conscious in man. By a neglect of interior submission, man fails of this antecedent, Unity; and as a consequence his attempts at union by exterior mastery have no success." Certain conditions are necessary to this, namely, the external arrangements indispensable *for* the evolution of the Uniting Spirit can alone be provided *by* the Uniting Spirit.

"We seem to be in an endless circle, of which both halves have lost their centre connexion; for it is an operation no less difficult than the junction of two such discs that is requisite to unity. These segments also being in motion, each upon a false centre of its own, the obstacles to union are incalculably multiplied.

"The spiritual or theoretic world in man revolves upon one set of principles, and the practical or actual world upon another. In ideality man recognises the purest truths, the highest notions of justice;—in actuality he departs from all these, and his entire career is confessedly a life of self-falseness and clever injustice. This barren ideality, and this actuality replete with bitter fruits, are the two hemispheres to be united for their mutual completion, and their common central point is the reality antecedent to them both. This point is not to be discovered by the rubbing of these two half globes together, by their curved sides, nor even as a school boy would attempt to unite his severed marble by the flat sides. The circle must be drawn anew from reality as a central point, the new radius embracing equally the new ideality and the new actuality.

"With this newness of love in men there would resplendently shine forth in them a newness of light, and a newness of life, charming the steadiest beholder." — *Introduction,* p. 4.

The remedy, which Mr. Lane proposes for the existing evils, is his "True Harmonic Association." But he more justly confides in "ceasing from doing" than in exhausting efforts at inadequate remedies. "From medicine to medicine is a change from disease to disease; and man must cease from self-activity, ere the spirit can fill him with truth in mind or health in body. The Civilization is become intensely false, and thrusts the human being into false predicaments. The antagonism of business to all that is high and good and generic is hourly declared by the successful, as well as by the failing. The mercantile system, based on individual aggrandizement, draws men from unity; its swelling columns of figures describe, in pounds, shillings, and pence, the degrees of man's departure from love, from wisdom, from power. The idle are as unhappy as the busy. Whether the dread factory-bell, or the fox-hunter's horn calls to a pursuit more fatal to man's best interests, is an inquiry which appears more likely to terminate in the cessation of both, than in a preference of either."

Mr. Lane does not confound society with sociableness. "On the contrary, it is when the sympathy with man is the stronger and the truer, that the sympathy with men grows weaker, and the sympathy with their actions weakest."

We must content ourselves with these few sentences from Mr. Lane's book, but we shall shortly hear from him again. This is no man of letters, but a man of ideas. Deep opens below deep in his thought, and for the solution of each new problem he recurs, with new success, to the highest truth, to that which is most generous, most simple, and most powerful; to that which cannot be comprehended, or overseen, or exhausted. His words come to us like the voices of home out of a far country.

With Mr. Lane is associated in the editorship of a monthly tract, called "The Healthian," and in other kindred enterprises, Mr. Henry G. Wright, who is the teacher of the School at Ham Common, near Richmond, and the author of several tracts on moral and social topics.

This school is founded on a faith in the presence of the Divine Spirit in man. The teachers say, "that in their first experiments they found they had to deal with a higher nature than the mere mechanical. They found themselves in contact with an essence indefinably delicate. The great difficulty with relation to the children, with which they were first called to wrestle, was an unwillingness to admit access to their spiritual natures. The teachers felt this keenly. They sought for the cause. They found it in their own hearts. Pure spirit would not, could not hold communion with their corrupted modes. These must be surrendered, and love substituted in lieu of them. The experience was soon made that the primal duty of the educator is entire self-surrender to love. Not partial, not of the individual, but pure, unlimited, universal. It is impossible to speak to natures deeper than those from which you speak. Reason cries to Reason, Love to Love. Hence the personal elevation of the teacher is of supreme importance." Mr. Alcott, who may easily be a little partial to an instructor who has adopted cordially his own methods, writes thus of his friend.

"Mr. Wright is a younger disciple of the same eternal verity, which I have loved and served so long. You have never seen his like, so deep serene, so clear, so true, and so good. His school is a most refreshing and happy place. The children are mostly under twelve years of age, of both sexes; and his art and method of education simple and natural. It seemed like being again in my own school, save that a wiser wisdom directs, and a lovelier love presides over its order and teachings. He is not yet thirty years of age, but he has more genius for education than any man I have seen, and not of children alone, but he possesses the rare art of teaching men and women. What I have dreamed, and stammered, and preached, and prayed about so long, is in him clear and definite. It is life, influence, reality. I flatter myself that I shall bring him with me on my return. He cherishes hopes of making our land the place of his experiment on human culture, and of proving to others the worth of the divine idea that now fills and exalts him."

In consequence of Mr. Greaves's persuasion, which seems to be shared by his friends, that the special remedy for the evils of society at the present moment is association; perhaps from a more universal tendency, which has drawn in many of the best minds in this country also to accuse the idealism, which contents itself with the history of the private mind, and to demand of every thinker the warmest dedication to the race, this class of which we speak are obviously inclined to favor the plans of the Socialists. They appear to be in active literary and practical connexion with Mr. Doherty, the intelligent and catholic editor of the London Phalanx, who is described to us as having been a personal friend of Fourier, and himself a man of sanguine temper, but a friend of temperate measures, and willing to carry his points with wise moderation, on one side; and in friendly relations with Robert Owen, "the philanthropist, 'who writes in brick and clay, in gardens and green fields,' who is a believer in the comforts and humanities of life, and would give these in abundance to all men," although they are widely distinguished from this last in their devout spiritualism. Many of the papers on our table contain schemes and hints for a better social organization, especially the plan of what they call "a Concordium, or a Primitive Home, which is about to be commenced by united individuals, who are desirous, under industrial and progressive education, with simplicity in diet, dress, lodging, &c., to retain the means for the harmonic development of their physical, intellectual, and moral natures." The institution is to be in the country, the inmates are to be of both sexes, they are to labor on the land, their drink is to be water, and their food chiefly uncooked by fire, and the habits of the members throughout of the same simplicity. Their unity is to be based on their education in a religious love, which subordinates all persons, and perpetually invokes the presence of the spirit in every transaction. It is through this tendency that these gentlemen have been drawn into fellowship with a humbler, but far larger class of their countrymen, of whom Goodwyn Barmby may stand for the representative.

Mr. Barmby is the editor of a penny magazine, called "The Promethean, or Communitarian Apostle," published monthly, and, as the covers inform us, "the cheapest of all magazines, and the paper the most devoted of any to the cause of the people; consecrated to Pantheism in Religion, and Communism in Politics." Mr. Barmby is a sort of Camille Desmoulins of British Revolution, a radical poet, with too little fear of grammar and rhetoric before his eyes, with as little fear of the Church or the State, writing often with as much fire, though not with as much correctness, as Ebenezer Elliott. He is the author of a poem called "The European Pariah," which will compare favorably with the Corn-law Rhymes. His paper is of great interest, as it details the conventions, the counsels, the measures of Barmby and his friends, for the organization of a new order of things, totally at war with the establishment. Its importance arises from the fact, that it comes obviously from the heart of the people. It is a cry of the miner and weaver for bread, for daylight, and fresh air, for space to exist in, and time to catch their breath and rest themselves in; a demand for political suffrage, and the power to tax as a counterpart to the liability of being taxed; a demand for leisure, for learning, for arts and sciences, for the higher social enjoyments. It is one of a cloud of pamphlets in the same temper and from the same quarter, which show a wholly new state of feeling in the body of the British people. In a time of distress among the manufacturing classes, severe beyond any precedent, when, according to the statements vouched by Lord Brougham in the House of Peers, and Mr. O'Connell and others in the Commons, wages are reduced in some of the manufacturing villages to six pence a week, so that men are forced to sustain themselves and their families at less than a penny a day; when the most revolting expedients are resorted to for food; when families attempt by a recumbent posture to diminish the pangs of hunger; in the midst of this exasperation the voice of the people is temperate and wise beyond all former example. They are intent on personal as well as on national reforms. Jack Cade leaves behind him his bludgeon and torch, and is grown amiable, literary, philosophical, and mystical. He reads Fourier, he reads Shelley, he reads Milton. He goes for temperance, for non-resistance, for education, and for the love-marriage, with the two poets above named; and for association, after the doctrines either of Owen or of Fourier. One of the most remarkable of the tracts before us is "A Plan for the Education and Improvement of the People, addressed to the Working-Classes of the United Kingdom; written in Warwick Gaol, by William Lovett, cabinet-maker, and John Collins, tool-maker," which is a calm, intelligent, and earnest plea for a new organization of the people, for the highest social and personal benefits, urging the claims of general education, of the Infant School, the Normal School, and so forth; announcing rights, but with equal emphasis admitting duties. And Mr. Barmby, whilst he attacks with great spirit and great contempt the conventions of society, is a worshipper of love and of beauty, and vindicates the arts. "The apostleship of veritable doctrine," he says, "in the fine arts is a really religious Apostolate, as the fine arts in their perfect manifestation tend to make mankind virtuous and happy."

It will give the reader some precise information of the views of the most devout and intelligent persons in the company we have described, if we add an account of a public conversation which occurred during the last summer. In the (London) Morning Chronicle, of 5 July, we find the following advertisement. "Public Invitation. An open meeting of the friends to human progress will be held to-morrow, July 6, at Mr. Wright's Alcott-House School, Ham Common, near Richmond, Surrey, for the purpose of considering and adopting means for the promotion of the great end, when all who are interested in human destiny are earnestly urged to attend. The chair taken at Three o'clock and again at Seven, by A. Bronson Alcott, Esq., now on a visit from America. Omnibuses travel to and fro, and the Richmond steam-boat reaches at a convenient hour."

Of this conference a private correspondent has furnished us with the following report.

A very pleasant day to us was Wednesday, the sixth of July. On that day an open meeting was held at Mr. Wright's Alcott-House School, Ham, Surrey, to define the aims and initiate the means of human culture. There were some sixteen or twenty of us assembled on the lawn at the back of the house. We came from many places; one 150 miles; another a hundred; others from various distances; and our brother Bronson Alcott from Concord, North America. We found it not easy to propose a question sufficiently comprehensive to unfold the whole of the fact with which our bosoms labored. We aimed at nothing less than to speak of the instauration of Spirit and its incarnation in a beautiful form. We had no chairman, and needed none. We came not to dispute, but to hear and to speak. And when a word failed in extent of meaning, we loaded the word with new meaning. The word did not confine our experience, but from our own being we gave significance to the word. Into one body we infused many lives, and it shone as the image of divine or angelic or human thought. For a word is a Proteus that means to a man what the man is. Three papers were successively presented.

I. REFORMATION

"Old things shall pass away."

That an integral reform will comprise, not only an amendment in our (1) Corn Laws, (2) Monetary Arrangements, (3) Penal Code, (4) Education, (5) the Church, (6) the Law of Primogeniture, (7) Divorce; but will extend to questions yet publicly unmooted, or unfavorably regarded, such as (1) that of a reliance on Commercial Prosperity, (2) a belief in the value of the purest conceivable Representative Legislature, (3) the right of man to inflict Pain on man, (4) the demand for a purer Generation in preference to a better Education, (5) the reign of Love in Man instead of human Opinions, (6) the restoration of all things to their primitive Owner, and hence the abrogation of Property, either individual or collective, and (7) the Divine Sanction, instead of the Civil and Ecclesiastical authority, for Marriage.

That the obstacles encountered, in any endeavor to secure the smallest proposed public reform, are not to be taken as a measure for the difficulties in realizing those of a deeper character, as above enumerated; for as the latter are more vital and real, so are they less dependent on public concurrence, and need rather an individual practice than an associative appeal.

That while the benevolent mind perceives and desires the entire reform which should be accomplished, the practical reformer will bound his aims by that which is *possible* at the moment; for while a twenty years' agitation is insufficient to procure the slightest modification in the Corn Laws, of little value when attained, and fifty years' advocacy shall not accomplish a reform in parliament, declared worthless and delusive as soon as it is conceded, the abiding, and real, and happy reforms are much more within our own power, at the same time that their value is, under every consideration, undoubted.

That however extensive, grand, or noble may be the ultimate measures proposed, it is thus the imperative duty of the sincere reformer at once to commence that course of conduct, which must not less conduce to his own than to the universal good.

That a reform in the relation of master and servant, in faith in money, in deference to wealth, in diet, habits of life, modes of intercourse, and other particulars, almost or entirely under the control of each individual, is the first series of practical measures to be adopted, at once the proof of sincerity, and the earnest of future success.

That a personal reform of this kind, humble as it may appear, is obviously the key to every future and wider good. By reformed individuals only can reformed laws be enacted, or reformed plans effected. By him alone, who is reformed and well regulated, can the appeal fairly be made to others, either privately or publicly, to submit to a superior rule. By such as have themselves become somewhat purified must the purer life and measures be indicated. The greatest Apostle of Reform is the most reformed.

The speaker added as a comment on this paper, Human institutions and human habits are but the histories of men's natures, and have in all times disclosed the heaven-wandering attributes of their projectors. At present, institutions are extremely complex, and so wreathed together, that one reform compels a hundred, and of course every attempt to reform in one part is resisted by the establishment in all parts. But the divine thought permits us not to remain in quietude. That, which we are not, rises before us, as that, which we are to be. Our aspirations are the pledge of their own fulfilment. Hope drives forward with the speed of wind, and affirms that the unallowable of to-day shall be to-morrow within our reach; if that which is to-day only attainable shall to-morrow be a realized fact.

Beneath the actual which a man is, there is always covered a possible to tempt him forward, and beneath that an impossible. Beneath sense lie reason and understanding; beneath them both, humility; and beneath all, God. To be Godlike, we must pass through the grades of progress. We may make the experiences of the rational the humane life, and at last the life of God. But our precessions are not so much of time as of being. Even now the God-life is enfolded in us, even now the streams of eternity course freely in our central heart. If impelled by the spirit to intermingle with the arrangements of polities of the world in order to improve them, we shall discover the high point, from which we begin by the God-thought, in our interference. Our act must be divine. We seem to do; God does. God empowers legislators, and ennobles them for their fidelity. Let them, however, be apostles, not apostles' representatives; men of God, not men of men. Personal elevation is our credentials. Personal reform is that which is practicable, and without it our efforts on behalf of others are dreams only.

After this had been considered and approved, another of our friends offered the following scripture.

II. TRANSITION

"Bring no more vain oblations."

As men sincerely desirous of *being* that which we have *conceived* in idea, earnestly longing to assert the transcendency of divine humanity over all creeds, sayings, and theories, the question occurred to us, "How shall we find bread for the support of our bodies?" We proposed reducing our wants to nature's simplest needs; but on due consideration, we perceived that the restrictions on food precluded our obtaining it, and we learned with dismay that the spirit, which monopolizes bread and other constituents of life, denounced from the bosom of society, "You shall not live a conscientious life."

Not abashed, however, by this decree, we resolved to press our investigations, and we asked who had uttered this practical blasphemy in the face of high heaven? And all voices answered, that "the men trusting in property had done it." We took up this question of property, and asked, "By what tenure is it held?" And society answered, "On the tenure of might and immemorial custom." But when we interrogated our own hearts, and asked, "Did Divinity ever thus sanction possession?" our hearts, indeed, answered not; but the God within spoke plainly, that "Pure Love, which is ever communicative; never yet conceded to any being the right of appropriation." But when society urged further, that government had legitimated possession, we began to inquire on what authority government itself rested. And the government's answer was immediately proffered, "We protect the rights of property, and devise means for the accumulation of more. We shield the good from adversities, and we punish the evil-doers." Is this true? we thought. . . . No; government had not redeemed its promise to us, and we would no longer care for its provisions. The first law, too, of Heaven is Love, and government is founded on force. We were not believers in force; we believed that moral majesty was far more protection to man than the shield of a mighty empire; — we believed that a man encased in his own humanity was more secure, than he who was protected by a thousand bayonets. Our faith was in moral uprightness, and not in the prowess of armies. We would be established in love, and not in fear; and government is, in all these respects, infidel to the good. We asked, "Whether domination was of God?" and God answered, "No."

But we thought that the religious institute would do something for humanity, that the priest would succor the oppressed, and loose the burdens of the heavy laden. But the priest told us, he too loved, above all things, domination and homage. . . . He laughed at human perfectibility. He declared, that loyalty to the prince, and pecuniary reverence to the church, were his only hope of salvation.

We, therefore, ignore human governments, creeds, and institutions; we deny the right of any man to dictate laws for our regulation, or duties for our performance; and declare our allegiance only to Universal Love, the all-embracing Justice.

In addition to this statement of his thought the second speaker asked, Why does a man need an outward law? Simply because the law of love has been hidden. Men, are they not bankers and capitalists, whose Bank and Capital is God? Why should they borrow of men? Why should the all-wealthy seek the substitutes of riches? If we assert our manhood, what do we need of learning, precedent, or government? Let the impoverished seek for notes of hand; let the timid and lawless ask protection of the arm of power. Let the foolish still dream, that the vanity of book-miners will be their wisdom for us, we claim wealth, love, and wisdom, as essential informations of the Divinity. Besides, human institutions bear no fruit. If you plant them, they will yield nothing. Prohibitions and commands stand for nothing. "Thou shalt not kill," which is a history recording to sense what the divine law of purity suggests in every unperverted heart, is held binding by none. What shall I not kill? asks the butcher, the poulterer, the fishmonger, and he answers, All things in which I do not trade. And what shall the soldier not kill? All men, except his enemies. These exceptions make the law nugatory. The command is universal only for the pure soul, that neither stabs nor strangles. The laws of men inculcate and command slaughter. Nor will they exculpate rebellion on the ground, that holiness has rendered obedience impossible. But we must ignore laws which ignore holiness. Our trust is in purity, not in vengeance.

A third person had written down his thought as follows.

III. FORMATION

"Behold I make all things new."

That in order to attain the highest excellence of which man is capable, not only is a searching Reform necessary in the existing order of men and things, but the Generation of a new race of persons is demanded, who shall project institutions and initiate conditions altogether original, and commensurate with the being and wants of humanity.

That the germs of this new generation are even now discoverable in human beings, but have been hitherto either choked by ungenial circumstances, or, having borne fruit prematurely or imperfectly, have attained no abiding growth.

That the elements for a superior germination consist in an innocent fertile mind, and a chaste healthful body, built up from the purest and most volatile productions of the uncontaminated earth; thus removing all hinderances to the immediate influx of Deity into the spiritual faculties and corporeal organs. Hence the true Generator's attention will be drawn to whatsoever pertains to the following constituents of Man and of Society: —

Primarily, Marriage and the Family Life, including of course, the Breeding and Education of Children.

Secondly, Housewifery and Husbandry.

Thirdly, The relations of the Neighborhood.

Fourthly, Man's relation to the Creator.

It is obvious, that society, as at present constituted, invades all and every one of these relations; and it is, therefore, proposed to select a spot whereon the new Eden may be planted, and man may, untempted by evil, dwell in harmony with his Creator, with himself, his fellows, and with all external natures.

On a survey of the present civilized world, Providence seems to have ordained the United States of America, more especially New England, as the field wherein this idea is to be realized in actual experience; and, trusting in the faith which inspires, the hope which ensures, and the power which enacts, a few persons, both in the new country and the old, are uniting their efforts to secure, at the earliest possible moment, and by the simplest possible means, a consummation so sublime, so humane, so divine.

After reading this paper, he added words to this effect. Reformation belongs not to us, it is but a chimera. We propose not to make new combinations of old substances, the elements themselves shall be new. The great enigma, to solve which man has ever labored, is answered in the one fact, Birth. The disciplines, the loves, the wishes, the sorrows, the joys, the travail of many years, are crowded into conception, gestation, and Birth. If you ask where evil commences, the answer is, in Birth. If you ask what is the unpardonable sin, the answer is an unholy birth. The most sacred, the most profane, the most solemn, the most irreverent, the most godlike, yet possibly the most brutal of acts. This one stands as a centre to all extremes, it is the point on which God and Devil wage most irreconcilable warfare. Let Birth be surrendered to the spirit, and the results shall be blessed.

Together with pure beings will come pure habits. A better body shall be built up from the orchard and the garden. The outward frame shall beam with soul; it shall be a vital fact in which is typically unfolded the whole of perfectness. As he who seizes on civil liberty with the hand of violence would act the tyrant, if power were entrusted to him, so he whose food is obtained by force or fraud would accomplish other purposes by similarly ignoble means. Tyranny and domination must be overcome, when they first take root in the lust of unhallowed things. From the fountain we will stake our thirst, and our appetite shall find supply in the delicious abundance that Pomona offers. Flesh and blood we will reject as "the accursed thing." A pure mind has no faith in them.

An unvitiated generation and more genial habits shall restore the Eden on Earth, and men shall again find that paradise is not merely a fable of the poets.

Such was the current of our thought; and most of those who were present felt delight in the conversations that followed. Said I not well, that it was a happy day? For though talk is never more than a portraiture of a fact, it may be, and ours was, the delineation of a fact based in the being of God.

THE DEATH OF DR. CHANNING

JANUARY, 1843

THE death of Dr. Channing at Bennington in Vermont, on the 2d October, is an event of great note to the whole country. The great loss of the community is mitigated by the new interest which intellectual power always acquires by the death of the possessor. Dr. Channing was a man of so much rectitude, and such power to express his sense of right, that his value to this country, of which he was a kind of public *Conscience*, can hardly be overestimated. Not only his merits, but his limitations also, which made all his virtues and talents intelligible and available for the correction and elevation of society, made our Cato dear, and his loss not to be repaired. His interest in the times, and the fidelity and independence, with which, for so many years, he had exercised that censorship on commercial, political, and literary morals, which was the spontaneous dictate of his character, had earned for him an accumulated capital of veneration, which caused his opinion to be waited for in each emergency, as that of the wisest and most upright of judges. We shall probably soon have an opportunity to give an extended account of his character and genius. In most parts of this country notice has been taken of this event, and in London also. Beside the published discourses of Messrs. Gannett, Hedge, Clarke, Parker, Pierpont, and Bellows, Mr. Bancroft made Dr. Channing's genius the topic of a just tribute in a lecture before the Diffusion Society at the Masonic Temple. We regret that the city has not yet felt the propriety of paying a public honor to the memory of one of the truest and noblest of its citizens.

TANTALUS

JANUARY, 1844

THE astronomers said, Give us matter and a little motion, and we will construct the universe. It is not enough that we should have matter, we must also have a single impulse, one shove to launch the mass, and generate the harmony of the centrifugal and centripetal forces. Once heave the ball from the hand, and we can show how all this mighty order grew.—A very unreasonable postulate, thought some of their students, and a plain begging of the question. Could you not prevail to know the genesis of projection as well as the continuation of it?—Nature, meantime, had not waited for the discussion, but, right or wrong, bestowed the impulse, and the balls rolled. It was no great affair, a mere push, but the astronomers were right in making much of it, for there is no end to the consequences of the act. That famous aboriginal push propagates itself through all the balls of the system, and through every atom of every ball; through all the races of creatures, and through the history and performances of every individual. Exaggeration is in the course of things. Nature sends no creature, no man, into the world, without adding a small excess of his proper quality. Given the planet, it is still necessary to add the impulse; so to every creature nature added a little violence of direction in its proper path, a shove to put it on its way; in every instance a slight generosity, a drop too much. Without electricity the air would rot, and without this violence of direction which men and women have, without a spice of bigot and fanatic, no excitement, no efficiency. We aim above the mark to hit the mark. Every act hath some falsehood of exaggeration in it. And when now and then comes along some sad, sharp-eyed man, who sees how paltry a game is played and refuses to play, but blabs the secret; how then? is the bird flown? O no, the wary Nature sends a new troop of fairer forms, of lordlier youths, with a little more excess of direction to hold them fast to their several aim; makes them a little wrong-headed in that direction in which they are rightest, and on goes the game again with new whirl for a generation or two more. See the child, the fool of his senses, with his thousand pretty pranks, commanded by every sight and sound, without any power to compare and rank his sensations, abandoned to every bauble, to a whistle, a painted chip, a lead dragoon, a gilt gingerbread horse; individualizing every thing, generalizing nothing, who thus delighted with every thing new, lies down at night overpowered by the fatigue, which this day of continual pretty madness has incurred. But Nature has answered her purpose with the curly, dimpled lunatic. She has tasked every faculty and has secured the symmetrical growth of the bodily frame by all these attitudes and exertions; an end of the first importance, which could not be trusted to any care less perfect than her own. This glitter, this opaline lustre plays round the top of every toy to his eye, to ensure his fidelity, and he is deceived to his good.

We are made alive and kept alive by the same arts. Let the stoics say what they please, we do not eat for the good of living, but because the meat is savory, and the appetite is keen. Nature does not content herself with casting from the flower or the tree a single seed, but she fills the air and earth with a prodigality of seeds, that, if thousands perish, thousands may plant themselves, that hundreds may come up, that tens may live to maturity, that at least one may replace the parent. All things betray the same calculated profusion. The excess of fear with which the animal frame is hedged round, shrinking from cold, starting at sight of a snake, at every sudden noise or falling stone, protects us through a multitude of groundless alarms from some one real danger at last. The lover seeks in marriage his private felicity and perfection, with no prospective end; and nature hides in his happiness her own end, namely, progeny, or the perpetuity of the race.

But the craft with which the world is made runs also into the mind and character of men. No man is quite sane, but each has a vein of folly in his composition, a slight determination of blood to the head, to make sure of holding him hard to some one point which nature had taken to heart.

Great causes are never tried on their merits; but the great cause is reduced to particulars, to suit the size of the partisans, and the contention is ever hottest on minor matters. Not less remarkable is that overfaith of each man in the importance of what he has to do or say. The poet, the prophet has a higher value for what he utters, than any hearer, and therefore it gets spoken. The strong, self-complacent Luther declares, with an emphasis not to be mistaken, that "God himself cannot do without wise men." Jacob Behmen and George Fox betray their egotism in the pertinacity of their controversial tracts, and James Naylor once suffered himself to be worshipped as the Christ. Each prophet comes presently to identify himself with his thought, and to esteem his hat and shoes sacred. However this may discredit such persons with the judicious, it helps them with the people, and gives pungency, heat, and publicity to their words. A similar experience is not infrequent in private life. Each young and ardent person writes a diary, into which, when the hours of prayer and penitence arrive, he inscribes his soul. The pages thus written are to him burning and fragrant; he reads them on his knees by midnight and by the morning star; he wets them with his tears. They are sacred; too good for the world, and hardly yet to be shown to the dearest friend. This is the man-child that is born to the soul, and her life still circulates in the babe. The living cord has not yet been cut. By and by, when some time has elapsed, he begins to wish to admit his friend or friends to this hallowed experience, and with hesitation, yet with firmness, exposes the pages to his eye. Will they not burn his eyes? The friend coldly turns them over, and returns from the writing to conversation with easy transition, which strikes the other party with astonishment and vexation. He cannot suspect the writing itself. Days and nights of fervid life, of communion with angels of darkness and of light, bear witness in his memory to that tear-stained book. He suspects the intelligence or the heart of his friend. Is there then no friend? He cannot yet credit that one may have impressive experience, and yet may not know how to put his private fact into literature, or into harmony with the great community of minds; and perhaps the discovery, that wisdom has other tongues and ministers than we, that the truth, which burns like living coals in our heart, burns in a thousand breasts, and though we should hold our peace, that would not the less be spoken, might check too suddenly the flames of our zeal. A man can only speak so long as he does not feel his speech to be partial and inadequate. It is partial, but he does not see it to be so whilst he makes it. As soon as he is released from the instinctive, the particular, and sees its partiality, he shuts his mouth in disgust. For no man can write any thing, who does not think that what he writes is for the time the history of the world; or do any thing well, who does not esteem his work to be of greatest importance. My work may be of none, but I must not think it of none, or I shall not do it with impunity.

In like manner, there is throughout nature something mocking, something that leads us on and on, but arrives nowhere, keeps no faith with us; all promise outruns the performance. We live in a system of approximations, not of fulfilment. Every end is prospective of some other end, which is also temporary; a round and final success nowhere. We are encamped in nature, not domesticated. Hunger and thirst lead us on to eat and to drink, but bread and wine, mix and cook them how you will, leave us hungry and thirsty after the stomach is full. It is the same with all our arts and performances. Our music, our poetry, our language itself, are not satisfactions but suggestions.

The pursuit of wealth, of which the results are so magical in the contest with nature, and in reducing the face of the planet to a garden, is like the headlong game of the children in its reaction on the pursuers. What is the end sought? Plainly to secure the ends of good sense and beauty from the intrusion of deformity or vulgarity of any kind. But men use a very operose method. What an apparatus of means to secure a little conversation! This great palace of brick and stone, these servants, this kitchen, these stables, horses, and equipage; this bankstock and file of mortgages; trade to all the world; countryhouse and cottage by the waterside; all for a little conversation, high, clear, and spiritual! Could it not be had as well by beggars on the highway? No, all these things came from the successive efforts of these beggars to remove one and another interference. Wealth was applied first to remove friction from the wheels of life; to give clearer opportunity. Conversation, character, were the avowed ends; wealth was good as it silenced the creaking door, cured the smoky chimney, brought friends together in a warm and quiet room, and kept the children and the dinner-table in a different apartment. Thought, virtue, beauty, were the ends, but it was known that men of thought and virtue sometimes had the headache, or wet feet, or could lose good time whilst the room was getting warm in winter days. Unluckily in the exertions necessary to remove these inconveniences, the main attention had been diverted to this object; the old aims had been lost sight of, and to remove friction had come to be the end. That is the ridicule of rich men, and Boston, London, Vienna, and now the governments generally of the world are *cities and governments of the rich,* and the masses are not men, but *poor men,* that is, men who would be rich; that is the ridicule of the class, that they arrive with pains and sweat, and fury, nowhere; when all is done, it is for nothing. They are men who have interrupted the whole conversation of a company to make their speech, and now have forgotten what they went to say. The appearance strikes the eye, everywhere, of an aimless society, an aimless nation, an aimless world. Were the ends of nature so great and cogent as to exact this immense sacrifice of men?

Quite analogous to these deceits in life, there is, as might be expected, a similar effect on the eye from the face of external nature. There is in woods and waters a certain enticement and flattery, together with a failure to yield a present satisfaction. This disappointment is felt in every landscape. I have seen the softness and beauty of the summer clouds floating feathery overhead, enjoying, as it seemed, their height and privilege of motion, whilst yet they appeared not so much the drapery of this place and hour, as fore-looking to some pavilions and gardens of festivity beyond. Who is not sensible of this jealousy? Often you shall find yourself not near enough to your object. The pine tree, the river, the bank of flowers, before you, does not seem to be nature. Nature is still elsewhere. This or this is but outskirt and far-off reflection and echo of the triumph that has passed by, and is now at its glancing splendor and heyday, perchance in the neighboring fields, or, if you stood in the field, then in the adjacent woods. The present object shall give you this sense of stillness that follows a pageant which has just gone by. It is the same among the men and women, as among the silent trees; always a referred existence, an absence, never a presence and satisfaction. Is it that beauty can never be grasped? in persons and in landscape is equally inaccessible? The accepted and betrothed lover has lost the wildest charm of his maiden in her acceptance of him. She was heaven whilst he pursued her as a star. She cannot be heaven if she stoops to such an one as he. So is it with these wondrous skies, and hills, and forests. What splendid distance, what recesses of ineffable pomp and loveliness in the sunset! But who can go where they are, or lay his land, or plant his foot thereon? Off they fall from the round world for ever and ever; glory is not for hands to handle.

What shall we say of this omnipresent appearance of that first projectile impulse, this flattery and baulking of so many good well-meaning creatures?

Must we not suppose somewhere in the universe a slight treachery, a slight derision? Are we not engaged to a serious resentment of this use that is made of us? Are we tickled trout, and fools of nature? Unhappily, there is not the smallest prospect of advantage from such considerations. Practically, there is no great danger of their being pressed. One look at the face of heaven and earth puts all petulance at rest, and soothes us to wiser convictions. We see that Nature converts itself into a vast promise, and will not be rashly explained. Her secret is untold. Many and many an Œdipus arrives; he has the whole mystery teeming in his brain. Alas! the same sorcery has spoiled his skill; no syllable can he shape on his lips. Her mighty orbit vaults like the fresh rainbow into the deep, but no archangel's wing was yet strong enough to follow it and report of the return of the curve. But it also appears, and the experience might dispose us to serenity, that our actions are seconded and disposed to greater conclusions than we designed. We are escorted on every hand through life by great spiritual potentates, and a beneficent purpose lies in wait for us. It is not easy to deal with Nature by card and calculation. We cannot bandy words with her; we cannot deal with her as man with man. If we measure our individual forces against hers, we may easily feel as if we were the sport of an overwhelming destiny. But if, instead of identifying ourselves with the work, we feel that the soul of the Workman streams through us, that a paradise of love and power lies close beside us, where the Eternal Architect broods on his thought and projects the world from his bosom, we may find the peace of the morning dwelling first in our hearts, and the fathomless powers of gravity and chemistry, and over them of life, pre-existing within us in their highest form.

ETHNICAL SCRIPTURES

April, 1844

CHALDÆAN ORACLES

We owe to that eminent benefactor of scholars and philosophers, the late Thomas Taylor, who, we hope, will not long want a biographer, the collection of the "Oracles of Zoroaster and the Theurgists," from which we extract all the sentences ascribed to Zoroaster, and a part of the remainder. We prefix a portion of Mr. Taylor's preface: —

"These remains of Chaldæan theology are not only venerable for their antiquity, but inestimably valuable for the unequalled sublimity of the doctrines they contain. They will doubtless, too, be held in the highest estimation by every liberal mind, when it is considered that some of them are the sources whence the sublime conceptions of Plato flowed, and that others are perfectly conformable to his most abstruse dogmas.

"I add, for the sake of those readers that are unacquainted with the scientific theology of the ancients, that as the highest principle of things is a nature truly ineffable and unknown, it is impossible that this visible world could have been produced by him without mediums; and this not through any impotency, but, on the contrary, through transcendency of power. For if he had produced all things without the agency of intermediate beings, all things must have been, like himself, ineffable and unknown. It is necessary, therefore, that there should be certain mighty powers between the supreme principle of things and us: for we, in reality, are nothing more than the dregs of the universe. These mighty powers, from their surpassing similitude to the first god, were very properly called by the ancients, gods; and were considered by them as perpetually subsisting in the most admirable and profound union with each other, and the first cause; yet so as amidst this union to preserve their own energy distinct from that of the highest god. For it would be absurd in the extreme, to allow that man has a peculiar energy of his own, and to deny that this is the case with the most exalted beings. Hence, as Proclus beautifully observes, the gods may be compared to trees rooted in the earth: for as these, by their roots, are united with the earth, and become earthly in an eminent degree, without being earth itself; so the gods, by their summits, are profoundly united to the first cause, and by this means are transcendently similar to, without being the first cause.

"Lines, too, emanating from the centre of a circle, afford us a conspicuous image of the manner in which these mighty powers proceed from, and subsist in, the ineffable principle of things. For here, the lines are evidently things different from the centre, to which, at the same time, by their summits, they are exquisitely allied. And these summits, which are indescribably absorbed in the centre, are yet no parts (*i. e.* powers) of it: for the centre has a subsistence prior to them, as being their cause."

ORACLES OF ZOROASTER

There is also a portion for the image [1] in the place [2] every way splendid.

[1] That is, the irrational soul, which is the image of the rational.

[2] That is, the region above the moon.

Nor should you leave the dregs of matter[1] in the precipice.[2]

Nor should you expel the soul from the body, lest in departing it retain something.[3]

[4] Direct not your attention to the immense measures of the earth; for the plant of truth is not in the earth. Nor measure the dimensions of the sun, by means of collected rules; for it revolves by the eternal will of the Father, and not for your sake. Dismiss the sounding course of the moon; for it perpetually runs through the exertions of necessity. The advancing procession of the stars was not generated for your sake. The wide-spread aërial wing of birds, and the sections of victims and viscera are never true; but all these are mere puerile sports, the foundations of mercantile deception. Fly from these, if you intend to open the sacred paradise of piety, where virtue, wisdom, and equity, are collected together.

Explore the river[5] of the soul, whence, or in what order, having become a servant to body, you may again rise to that order from which you flowed, uniting operation to *sacred* reason.[6]

Verge not downward, a precipice lies under the earth, which draws through a descent of seven steps,[7]

[1] *i. e.* The human body.

[2] *i. e.* This terrestrial region.

[3] *i. e.* Lest it retain something of the more passive life.

[4] This oracle is conformable to what Plato says in his Republic, that a philosopher must astronomize above the heavens: that is to say, he must speculate the celestial orbs, as nothing more than images of forms in the intelligible world.

[5] *i. e.* The producing cause of the soul.

[6] By sacred reason, is meant the summit, or principal power of the soul, which Zoroaster, in another place, calls the flower of intellect.

[7] *i. e.* The orbs of the seven planets.

and under which lies the throne of dire necessity.

You should never change barbarous names.[1]

In a certain respect, the world possesses intellectual, inflexible sustainers.[2]

Energize about the Hecatic sphere.[3]

If you invoke *me*,[4] all things will appear to you to be a lion. For neither will the convex bulk of heaven then be visible; the stars will not shine; the light of the moon will be concealed; the earth will not stand firm; but all things will be seen in thunder.

On all sides, with an unfigured[5] soul, extend the reins of fire.

O man, thou subtle production,[6] that art of a bold nature!

In the left hand inward parts of Hecate[7] is the

[1] For in every nation there are names of divine origin, and which possess an ineffable power in mystic operations.

[2] *i. e.* The fontal fathers, or intellectual gods. By *inflexible*, understand stable power.

[3] This sphere was of gold. In the middle of it there was a sapphire; and the sphere itself was turned round by means of a thong, made of the hide of an ox. It was likewise every where inscribed with characters; and the Chaldæans turning it round, made certain invocations. But it is called Hecatine, because dedicated to Hecate.

[4] By *me* is meant the fountain or cause of the celestial constellation called the lion.

[5] By *unfigured*, understand most simple and pure; and by the reins of fire, the unimpeded energy of the theurgic life of such a soul.

[6] Man is a *subtle* production, considered as the work of the *secret* art of divinity. But he is of a bold nature, as exploring things more excellent than himself.

[7] Hecate, according to the Chaldæans, is the centre of the intellectual gods: and they say, that in her right hand parts she contains the fountain of souls; and in her left, the fountain of the virtues.

fountain of virtue, which wholly abides within, and does not emit its virginal nature.

When you behold a sacred fire[1] without form, shining with a leaping splendor through the profundities of the whole world, hear the voice of fire.

You should not invoke the self-conspicuous image of nature.[2]

Nature persuades us that there are holy dæmons, and that the blossoms of depraved matter[3] are useful and good.

[4] The soul of mortals compels, in a certain respect, divinity into itself, possessing nothing mortal, and is wholly inebriated from deity; for it glories in the harmony[5] under which the mortal body subsists.

The immortal depth[6] of the soul should be the leader; but vehemently extend all your eyes[7] upwards.

You should not defile the spirit,[8] nor give depth to a superficies.

Seek Paradise.[9]

[1] This oracle relates to the vision of divine light.

[2] *i. e.* The image, to be invoked in the mysteries, must be intelligible, and not sensible.

[3] By the blossoms of depraved matter, understand the dæmons called *Evil;* but which are not so essentially, but from their office.

[4] That is, the human soul, through its immortality and purity, becomes replete with a more excellent life, and divine illumination; and is, as it were, raised above itself.

[5] *i. e.* Unapparent and intelligible harmony.

[6] *i. e.* The summit or flower of its nature.

[7] *i. e.* All the gnostic powers of the soul.

[8] Understand by the *spirit,* the aërial vehicle of the soul; and by the *superficies,* the ethereal and lucid vehicle.

[9] The Chaldaic Paradise is the choir of divine powers about the Father of the universe; and the empyrean beauties of the demiurgic fountains.

[1] The wild beasts of the earth shall inhabit thy vessel.

By extending a fiery intellect[2] to the work of piety, you will also preserve the flowing body.

From the bosom therefore of the earth, terrestrial dogs[3] leap forth, who never exhibit a true sign to mortal man.

The Father[4] perfected all things, and delivered them to the second intellect,[5] which the nations of men call the first.

The furies are the bonds of men.[6]

The paternal intellect disseminated symbols[7] in souls.

[8] Those souls that leave the body with violence are the most pure.

The soul being a splendid fire, through the power of the father remains immortal, is the mistress[9] of life, and possesses many perfections of the bosoms of the world.

[1] By the vessel is meant the composite temperature of the soul; and by the wild beasts of the earth, terrestrial dæmons. These, therefore, will reside in the soul which is replete with irrational affections.

[2] *i. e.* An intellect full of divine light.

[3] *i. e.* Material dæmons.

[4] *i. e.* Saturn.

[5] *i. e.* Jupiter.

[6] That is, the powers that punish guilty souls, bind them to their material passions, and in these, as it were, suffocate them; such punishment being finally the means of purification. Nor do these powers only afflict the vicious, but even such as convert themselves to an immaterial essence; for these, through their connection with matter, require a purification of this kind.

[7] That is, symbols of all the divine natures.

[8] This oracle praises a violent death, because the soul, in this case, is induced to hate the body, and rejoice in a liberation from it.

[9] The soul is the mistress of life, because it extends vital illuminations to the body, which is, of itself, destitute of life.

The Father did not hurl forth fear, but infused persuasion.[1]

The Father [2] has hastily withdrawn himself, but has not shut up his proper fire, in his own intellectual power.

There is a certain intelligible [3] which it becomes you to understand with the flower of intellect.

The expelling powers [4] of the soul which cause her to respire, are of an unrestrained nature.

It becomes you to hasten to the light and the rays of the Father, whence a soul was imparted to you, invested with an abundance of intellect.

All things are the progeny of one fire. [5]

[6] That which intellect says, it undoubtedly says by intellection.

[7] Ha! ha! the earth from beneath bellows at these as far as to their children.

You should not increase your fate.[8]

[1] That is, as divinity is not of a tyrannical nature, he draws every thing to himself by persuasion, and not by fear.

[2] That is, Saturn, the summit of the intellectual order, is perfectly separated from all connection with matter; but, at the same time, imparts his divinity to inferior natures.

[3] Meaning the intelligible, which immediately subsists after the highest God.

[4] That is, those powers of the soul which separate it from the body.

[5] That is, of one divine nature.

[6] That is, the voice of intellect is an intellectual, or, in other words, an immaterial and indivisible energy.

[7] The meaning of the oracle is, that even the very children of the impious are destined to subterranean punishments; and this, with the greatest propriety; for those who, in a former life, have perpetrated similar crimes, become, through the wise administration of Providence, the members of one family.

[8] *Fate* is the full perfection of those divine illuminations which are received by *Nature;* but *Providence* is the immediate energy of deity. Hence, when we energize intellectually, we are under the dominion of Providence; but when corporeally, under that

Nothing imperfect proceeds, according to a circular energy, from a paternal principle.[1]

But the paternal intellect will not receive the will of the soul, till she has departed from oblivion;[2] and has spoken the word, assuming the memory of her paternal sacred impression.

When you behold the terrestrial[3] dæmon approaching, vociferate and sacrifice the stone MNIZURIM.

Learn the intelligible, for it subsists beyond intellect.[4]

The intelligible Iynges possess intellection themselves from the Father, so far as they energize intellectually, being moved by ineffable counsels.

He who knows himself, knows all things in himself, as Zoroaster first asserted, and afterwards Plato in the first Alcibiades.—*Pici Mirand. Op. tom.* 1, *p.* 211.

Since the soul perpetually runs, in a certain space of time it passes through all things, which circulation

of Fate. The oracle, therefore, admonishes to withdraw ourselves from corporeal energy.

[1] For divinity is self-perfect; and the imperfect cannot proceed from the perfect.

[2] That is, till she has recovered her knowledge of the divine symbols, and sacred reasons, from which she is composed; the former of which she receives from the divine unities, and the latter from sacred ideas.

[3] Terrestrial dæmons are full of deceit, as being remote from divine knowledge, and replete with dark matter; he, therefore, who desires to receive any true information from one of these, must prepare an altar, and sacrifice the stone *Mnizurim,* which has the power of causing another greater dæmon to appear, who, approaching invisible to the material dæmon, will give a true answer to the proposed question; and this to the interrogator himself.

[4] The intelligible is twofold; one kind being coördinate with intellect, but the other being of a super-essential characteristic.

being accomplished, it is compelled to run back again through all things, and unfold the same web of generation in the world, according to Zoroaster; who is of opinion, that the same causes, on a time returning, the same effects will, in a similar manner, return. — *Ficin. de Immortal. Anim. p.* 123.

ORACLES BY THE THEURGISTS

Our voluntary sorrows germinate in us as the growth of the particular life we lead.

On beholding yourself, fear.

Believe yourself to be above body, and you are.

Those robust souls perceive truth through themselves, and are of a more inventive nature; such a soul being saved through its own strength.

We should fly from the multitude of men going along in a herd.

The powers build up the body of a holy man.

Not knowing that every god is good, ye are fruitlessly vigilant.

Fiery hope should nourish you in the angelic region.

Ascending souls sing pæan.

To the persevering mortal the blessed immortals are swift.

All things are governed and subsist in faith, truth, and love.

The oracle says, Divinity is never so much turned away from man, and never so much sends him in novel paths, as when we make an ascent to the most divine of speculations or works, in a confused and disordered manner, and, as it adds, with unhallowed lips or unbathed feet. For, of those who are thus negligent, the progressions are imperfect, the impulses are vain, and the paths are blind.

The orders prior to Heaven possess mystic silence.

Every intellect apprehends deity.

The intelligible is food to that which understands.

You will not apprehend it by an intellectual energy as when understanding some particular thing.

It is not proper to understand that intelligible with vehemence, but with the extended flame of an extended intellect; a flame which measures all things, except that intelligible. But it is requisite to understand this. For if you incline your mind, you will understand it, though not vehemently. It becomes you therefore, bringing with you the pure convertible eye of your soul, to extend the void intellect to the intelligible, that you may learn its nature, because it has a subsistence above intellect.

SAYINGS OF PYTHAGORAS AND OF THE PYTHAGORIANS

Follow God.

All things are possible to the Gods.

Choose the most excellent life, and custom will make it pleasant.

This is the law of God, that virtue is the only thing that is strong.

Abstain from such things as are an impediment to prophecy, or to the purity and chastity of the soul, or to the habit of temperance or of virtue.

It is necessary to beget children, for it is necessary to leave those that may worship the Gods after us.

Other compacts are engraved in tables and pillars, but those with wives are inserted in children.

It is holy for a woman, after having been connected with her husband, to perform sacred rites on the same day, but this is never holy after she has been connected with any other man.

It is requisite to be silent, or to say something better than silence.

The possessions of friends are common.

The animal which is not naturally noxious to the human race should neither be injured nor slain.

Intoxication is the meditation of insanity.

The beginning is the half of the whole.

An oath should be taken religiously, since that which is behind is long.

Be sober, and remember to be disposed to believe, for these are the nerves of wisdom.

All the parts of human life, in the same manner as those of a statue, ought to be beautiful.

When the wise man opens his mouth, the beauties of his soul present themselves to the view, like the statues in a temple.

BOOK REVIEWS FROM THE DIAL

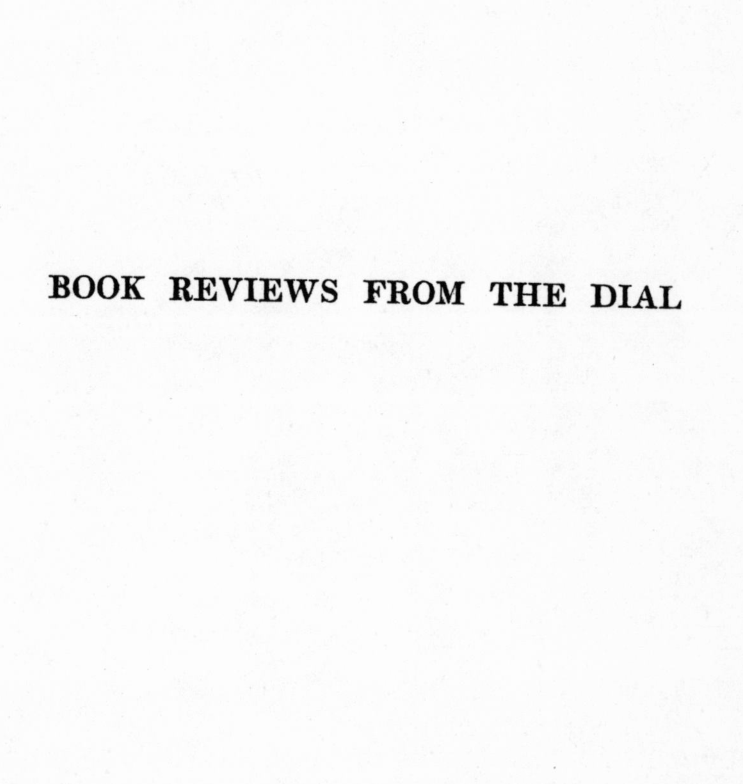

REVIEWS OF BOOKS

OCTOBER, 1840, TO OCTOBER, 1843

New Poetry

THE tendencies of the times are so democratical, that we shall soon have not so much as a pulpit or raised platform in any church or townhouse, but each person, who is moved to address any public assembly, will speak from the floor. The like revolution in literature is now giving importance to the portfolio over the book. Only one man in the thousand may print a book, but one in ten or one in five may inscribe his thoughts, or at least with short commentary his favorite readings in a private journal. The philosophy of the day has long since broached a more liberal doctrine of the poetic faculty than our fathers held, and reckons poetry the right and power of every man to whose culture justice is done. We own that, though we were trained in a stricter school of literary faith, and were in all our youth inclined to the enforcement of the straitest restrictions on the admission of candidates to the Parnassian fraternity, and denied the name of poetry to every composition in which the workmanship and the material were not equally excellent, in our middle age we have grown lax, and have learned to find pleasure in verses of a ruder strain, — to enjoy *verses of society,* or those effusions which in persons of a happy nature are the easy and unpremeditated translation of their thoughts and feelings into rhyme. This new taste for a certain private and household poetry, for somewhat less pretending than the festal and solemn verses which are written for the nations, really indicates, we suppose, that a new style of poetry exists. The number of writers has increased. Every child has been taught the tongues. The universal communication of the arts of reading and writing has brought the works of the great poets into every house, and made all ears familiar with the poetic forms. The progress of popular institutions has favored self-respect, and broken down that terror of the great, which once imposed awe and hesitation on the talent of the masses of society. A wider epistolary intercourse ministers to the ends of sentiment and reflection than ever existed before; the practice of writing diaries is becoming almost general; and every day witnesses new attempts to throw into verse the experiences of private life.

What better omen of true progress can we ask than an increasing intellectual and moral interest of men in each other? What can be better for the republic than that the Capitol, the White House, and the Court House are becoming of less importance than the farm-house and the book-closet? If we are losing our interest in public men, and finding that their spell lay in number and size only, and acquiring instead a taste for the depths of thought and emotion, as they may be sounded in the soul of the citizen or the countryman, does it not replace man for the state, and character for official power? Men should be treated with solemnity; and when they come to chant their private griefs and doubts and joys, they have a new scale by which to compute magnitude and relation. Art is the noblest consolation of calamity. The poet is compensated for his defects in the street and in society, if in his chamber he has turned his mischance into noble numbers.

Is there not room then for a new department in poetry, namely, *Verses of the Portfolio?* We have fancied that we drew greater pleasure from some manuscript verses than from printed ones of equal talent. For there was herein the charm of character; they were confessions; and the faults, the imperfect parts, the fragmentary verses, the halting rhymes, had a worth beyond that of a high finish; for they testified that the writer was more man than artist, more earnest than vain; that the thought was too sweet and sacred to him, than that he should suffer his ears to hear or his eyes to see a superficial defect in the expression.

The characteristic of such verses is, that being not written for publication, they lack that finish which the conventions of literature require of authors. But if poetry of this kind has merit, we conceive that the prescription which demands a rhythmical polish may be easily set aside; and when a writer has outgrown the state of thought which produced the poem, the interest of letters is served by publishing it imperfect, as we preserve studies, torsos, and blocked statues of the great masters. For though we should be loath to see the wholesome conventions, to which we have alluded, broken down by a general incontinence of publication, and every man's and woman's diary flying into the bookstores, yet it is to be considered, on the other hand, that men of genius are often more incapable than others of that elaborate execution which criticism exacts. Men of genius in general are, more than others, incapable of any perfect exhibition, because, however agreeable it may be to them to act on the public, it is always a secondary aim. They are humble, self-accusing, moody men, whose worship is toward the Ideal Beauty, which chooses to be courted not so often in perfect hymns, as in wild ear-piercing ejaculations, or in silent musings. Their face is forward, and their heart is in this heaven. By so much are they disqualified for a perfect success in any particular performance to which they can give only a divided affection. But the man of talents has every advantage in the competition. He can give that cool and commanding attention to the thing to be done, that shall secure its just performance. Yet are the failures of genius better than the victories of talent; and we are sure that some crude manuscript poems have yielded us a more sustaining and a more stimulating diet, than many elaborated and classic productions.

We have been led to these thoughts by reading some verses, which were lately put into our hands by a friend with the remark, that they were the production of a youth, who had long passed out of the mood in which he wrote them, so that they had become quite dead to him. Our first feeling on reading them was a lively joy. So then the Muse is neither dead nor dumb, but has found a voice in these cold Cisatlantic States. Here is poetry which asks no aid of magnitude or number, of blood or crime, but finds theatre enough in the first field or brookside, breadth and depth enough in the flow of its own thought. Here is self-repose, which to our mind is stabler than the Pyramids; here is self-respect which leads a man to date from his heart more proudly than from Rome. Here is love which sees through surface, and adores the gentle nature and not the costume. Here is religion, which is not of the Church of England, nor of the Church of Boston. Here is the good wise heart, which sees that the end of culture is strength and cheerfulness. In an age too which tends with so strong an inclination to the philosophical muse, here is poetry more purely intellectual than any American verses we have yet seen, distinguished from all competition by two merits; the fineness of perception; and the poet's trust in his own genius to that degree, that there is an absence of all conventional imagery, and a bold use of that which the moment's mood had made sacred to him, quite careless that it might be sacred to no other, and might even be slightly ludicrous to the first reader.

We proceed to give our readers some selections, taken without much order from this rich pile of manuscript. We first find the poet in his boat.

BOAT - SONG

The River calmly flows,
Through shining banks, through lonely glen,
Where the owl shrieks, though ne'er the cheer of men
Has stirred its mute repose,
Still if you should walk there, you would go there again.

The stream is well alive:
Another passive world you see,
Where downward grows the form of every tree;
Like soft light clouds they thrive:
Like them let us in our pure loves reflected be.

A yellow gleam is thrown
Into the secrets of that maze
Of tangled trees, which late shut out our gaze,
Refusing to be known;
It must its privacy unclose, — its glories blaze.

Sweet falls the summer air
Over her frame who sails with me:
Her way like that is beautifully free,
Her nature far more rare,
And is her constant heart of virgin purity.

A quivering star is seen
Keeping his watch above the hill,
Though from the sun's retreat small light is still
Poured on earth's saddening mien: —
We all are tranquilly obeying Evening's will.

Thus ever love the Power;
To simplest thoughts dispose the mind;
In each obscure event a worship find
Like that of this dim hour, —
In lights, and airs, and trees, and in all human kind.

We smoothly glide below
The faintly glimmering worlds of light:
Day has a charm, and this deceptive night
Brings a mysterious show; —
He shadows our dear earth, — but his cool stars are white.

Is there any boat-song like this? any in which the harmony proceeds so manifestly from the poet's mind, giving to nature more than it receives? In the following stanzas the writer betrays a certain habitual worship of genius, which characterizes many pieces in the collection, breaking out sometimes into very abrupt expression.

OCTOBER

Dry leaves with yellow ferns, — they are
Fit wreath of Autumn, while a star
Still, bright, and pure, our frosty air
Shivers in twinkling points
Of thin celestial hair,
And thus one side of heaven anoints.

I am beneath the moon's calm look
Most quiet in this sheltered nook
From trouble of the frosty wind
Which curls the yellow blade;
Though in my covered mind
A grateful sense of change is made.

To wandering men how dear this sight
Of a cold tranquil autumn night,
In its majestic deep repose;
    Thus will their genius be
    Not buried in high snows,
Though of as mute tranquillity.

An anxious life they will not pass,
Nor, as the shadow on the grass,
Leave no impression there to stay;
    To them all things are thought;
    The blushing morn's decay, —
Our death, our life, by this is taught.

O find in every haze that shines,
A brief appearance without lines,
A single word, — no finite joy;
    For present is a Power
    Which we may not annoy,
Yet love him stronger every hour.

I would not put this sense from me,
If I could some great sovereign be;
Yet will not task a fellow man
    To feel the same glad sense,
    For no one living can
Feel — save his given influence.

WILLINGNESS

An unendeavoring flower, — how still
Its growth from morn to eventime;
Nor signs of hasty anger fill
Its tender form from birth to prime
        Of happy will.

And some, who think these simple things
Can bear no goodness to their minds,
May learn to feel how nature brings,
Around a quiet being winds,
        And through us sings.

A stream to some is no delight,
Its element diffused around;
Yet in its unobtrusive flight
There trembles from its heart a sound
Like that of night.

So give thy true allotment, — fair;
To children turn a social heart;
And if thy days pass clear as air,
Or friends from thy beseeching part,
O humbly bear.

SONNETS

The brook is eddying in the forest dell,
All full of untaught merriment, — the joy
Of breathing life is this green wood's employ.
The wind is feeling through his gentle bell; —
I and my flowers receive this music well.
Why will not man his natural life enjoy?
Can he then with his ample spirit toy?
Are human thoughts as wares now baked to sell?
All up, all round, all down, a thrilling deep,
A holy infinite salutes the sense,
And incommunicable praises leap,
Shooting the entire soul with love intense,
Throughout the All, — and can a man live on to weep?

II.

There never lived a man who with a heart
Resolved, bound up, concentred in the good,
However low or high in rank he stood,
But when from him yourself had chanced to start,
You felt how goodness alway maketh art;
And that an ever venerable mood
Of sanctity, like the deep worship of a wood,
Of its unconsciousness turns you a part.

Let us live amply in the joyous All;
We surely were not meant to ride the sea,
Skimming the wave in that so prisoned Small,
Reposing our infinite faculties utterly.
Boom like a roaring sunlit waterfall,
Humming to infinite abysms; — speak loud, speak free.

III.

Hearts of eternity, — hearts of the deep!
Proclaim from land to sky your mighty fate;
How that for you no living comes too late;
How ye cannot in Theban labyrinth creep;
How ye great harvests from small surface reap;
Shout, excellent band, in grand primeval strain,
Like midnight winds that foam along the main,
And do all things rather than pause to weep.
A human heart knows nought of littleness,
Suspects no man, compares with no man's ways,
Hath in one hour most glorious length of days,
A recompense, a joy, a loveliness,
Like eaglet keen, shoots into azure far,
And always dwelling nigh is the remotest star.

LINES

WRITTEN IN THE EVENING OF A NOVEMBER DAY

Thee, mild autumnal day,
I felt not for myself; the winds may steal
From any point, and seem to me alike
Reviving, soothing powers.

Like thee the contrast is
Of a new mood in a decaying man,
Whose idle mind is suddenly revived
With many pleasant thoughts.

Our earth was gratified;
Fresh grass, a stranger in this frosty time,
Peeped from the crumbling mould as welcome as
An unexpected friend.

How glowed the evening star,
As it delights to glow in summer's midst,
When out of ruddy boughs the twilight birds
Sing flowing harmony.

Peace was the will to-day,
Love in bewildering growth our joyous minds
Swelled to their widest bounds; the worldly left
All hearts to sympathize.

I felt for thee, — for thee,
Whose inward, outward life completely moves,
Surrendered to the beauty of the soul
Of this creative day.

OUR BIRTH DAYS

I.

These are the solemnest days of our bright lives,
When memory and hope within exert
Delightful reign; when sympathy revives,
And that, which late was in the soul inert,
Grows warm and living, and to us alone
Are these a knowledge; nowise may they hurt,
Or cry aloud, or frighten out the tone,
Which we will strive to wear and as calm nature own.

II.

Whatever scenes our eyes once gratified, —
Those landscapes couched around our early homes,
To which our tender, peaceful hearts replied,
To those our present happy feeling roams,
And takes a mightier joy than from the tomes
Of the pure scholar; those ten thousand sights
Of constant nature flow in us, as foams
The bubbling spring; these are the true delights
Wherewith this solemn world the sorrowful requites.

These are proper Manuscript inspirations, honest, great, but crude. They have never been filed or decorated for the eye that studies surface. The writer was not afraid to write ill; he had a great meaning too much at heart to stand for trifles, and wrote lordly for his peers alone. This is the poetry of hope. Here is no French correctness, but Hans Sachs and Chaucer rather. But the minstrel can be sweet and tender also. We select from the sheaf one leaf, for which we predict a more general popularity.

A POET'S LOVE

I can remember well
My very early youth,
My sumptuous Isabel,
Who was a girl of truth,
Of golden truth; — we do not often see
Those whose whole lives have only known to be.

So sunlight, very warm,
On harvest fields and trees,
Could not more sweetly form
Rejoicing melodies
For these deep things, than Isabel for me;
I lay beneath her soul as a lit tree.

That cottage where she dwelt
Was all o'er mosses green;
I still forever felt
How nothing stands between
The soul and truth; why, starving poverty
Was nothing — nothing, Isabel, to thee.

Grass beneath her faint tread
Bent pleasantly away;
From her ne'er small birds fled,
But kept at their bright play,
Not fearing her; it was her endless motion,
Just a true swell upon a summer ocean.

Those who conveyed her home,—
I mean who led her where
The spirit does not roam,—
Had such small weight to bear,
They scarcely felt; how softly was thy knell
Rung for thee that soft day, girl Isabel.

I am no more below,
My life is raised on high;
My fantasy was slow
Ere Isabel could die;
It pressed me down; but now I sail away
Into the regions of exceeding day.

And Isabel and I
Float on the red brown clouds,
That amply multiply
The very constant crowds
Of serene shapes. Play on, Mortality!
Thy happiest hour is that when thou may'st die.

The second of the two following verses is of such extreme beauty, that we do not remember anything more perfect in its kind. Had the poet been looking over a book of Raffaelle's drawings, or perchance the villas and temples of Palladio, with the maiden to whom it was addressed?

TO * * * *

My mind obeys the power
That through all persons breathes;
And woods are murmuring,
And fields begin to sing,
And in me nature wreathes.

Thou too art with me here,—
The best of all design;—
Of that strong purity,
Which makes it joy to be
A distant thought of thine.

But here are verses in another vein, — plain, ethical, human, such as in ancient lands legislators carved on stone tablets and monuments at the roadside, or in the precincts of temples. They remind us of the austere strain in which Milton celebrates the Hebrew prophets.

> " In them is plainest taught and easiest learned
> What makes a nation happy and keeps it so."

I

The Bible is a book worthy to read;
The life of those great Prophets was the life we need,
From all delusive seeming ever freed.

Be not afraid to utter what thou art;
'Tis no disgrace to keep an open heart;
A soul free, frank, and loving friends to aid,
Not even does this harm a gentle maid.

Strive as thou canst, thou wilt not value o'er
Thy life. Thou standest on a lighted shore,
And from the waves of an unfathomed sea,
The noblest impulses flow tenderly to thee;
Feel them as they arise, and take them free.

Better live unknown,
No heart but thy own
Beating ever near,
To no mortal dear
In thy hemisphere,
Poor and wanting bread,
Steeped in poverty,
Than to be a dread,
Than to be afraid,
From thyself to flee;
For it is not living
To a soul believing,
To change each noble joy
Which our strength employs,

For a state half rotten
And a life of toys.
Better be forgotten
Than lose equipoise.

How shall I live? In earnestness.
What shall I do? Work earnestly.
What shall I give? A willingness.
What shall I gain? Tranquillity.
But do you mean a quietness
In which I act and no man bless?
Flash out in action infinite and free,
Action conjoined with deep tranquillity,
Resting upon the soul's true utterance,
And life shall flow as merry as a dance.

II

Life is too good to waste, enough to prize;
Keep looking round with clear unhooded eyes;
Love all thy brothers, and for them endure
Many privations; the reward is sure.

A little thing! There is no little thing;
Through all a joyful song is murmuring;
Each leaf, each stem, each sound in winter drear
Has deepest meanings for an anxious ear.

Thou seest life is sad; the father mourns his wife and child;
Keep in the midst of heavy sorrows a fair aspect mild.

A howling fox, a shrieking owl,
A violent distracting Ghoul,
Forms of the most infuriate madness,—
These may not move thy heart to gladness,
But look within the dark outside,
Nought shalt thou hate and nought deride.

Thou meet'st a common man
With a delusive show of *can*.
His acts are petty forgeries of natural greatness,
That show a dreadful lateness
Of this life's mighty impulses; a want of truthful earnestness;

He seems, not does, and in that shows
No true nobility,—
A poor ductility,
That no proper office knows,
Not even estimation small of human woes.

Be not afraid,
His understanding aid
With thy own pure content,
On highest purpose bent.

Leave him not lonely,
For that his admiration
Fastens on self and seeming only;
Make a right dedication
Of all thy strength to keep
From swelling that so ample heap
Of lives abused, of virtue given for nought,
And thus it shall appear for all in nature hast thou wrought.
If thou unconsciously perform what's good,
Like nature's self thy proper mood.

A life well spent is like a flower,
That had bright sunshine its brief hour;
It flourished in pure willingness;
Discovered strongest earnestness;
Was fragrant for each lightest wind;
Was of its own particular kind;—
Nor knew a tone of discord sharp;
Breathed alway like a silver harp;
And went to immortality
A very proper thing to die.

We will close our extracts from this rare file of blotted paper with a lighter strain, which, whilst it shows how gaily a poet can chide, gives us a new insight into his character and habits.

TORMENTS

Yes! they torment me
Most exceedingly:—
I would I could flee.
A breeze on a river—

I listen forever;
The yellowish heather
Under cool weather, —
These are pleasures to me.

What do torment me?
Those living vacantly,
Who live but to see;
Indefinite action,
Nothing but motion,
Round stones a rolling,
No inward controlling; —
Yes! they torment me.

Some cry all the time,
Even in their prime
Of youth's flushing clime.
O! out on this sorrow!
Fear'st thou to-morrow?
Set thy legs going,
Be stamping, be rowing, —
This of life is the lime.

Hail, thou mother Earth!
Who gave me thy worth
For my portion at birth:
I walk in thy azure,
Unfond of erasure,
But they who torment me
So most exceedingly
Sit with feet on the hearth.

We have more pages from the same hand lying before us, marked by the same purity and tenderness and early wisdom as these we have quoted, but we shall close our extracts here. May the right hand that has so written never lose its cunning! may this voice of love and harmony teach its songs to the too long silent echoes of the Western Forest.

Two Years before the Mast. A Personal Narrative of Life at Sea. New York: Harper and Brothers. 12mo, pp. 483.

This is a voice from the forecastle. Though a narrative of literal, prosaic truth, it possesses something of the romantic charm of Robinson Crusoe. Few more interesting chapters of the literature of the sea have ever fallen under our notice. The author left the halls of the University for the deck of a merchant vessel, exchanging " the tight dress coat, silk cap, and kid gloves of an undergraduate at Cambridge, for the loose duck trowsers, checked skirt, and tarpaulin hat of a sailor," and here presents us the fruits of his voyage. His book will have a wide circulation; it will be praised in the public prints; we shall be told that it does honor to his head and heart; but we trust that it will do much more than this; that it will open the eyes of many to the condition of the sailor, to the fearful waste of man, by which the luxuries of foreign climes are made to increase the amount of commercial wealth. This simple narrative, stamped with deep sincerity, and often displaying an unstudied, pathetic eloquence, may lead to reflections, which mere argument and sentimental appeals do not call forth. It will serve to hasten the day of reckoning between society and the sailor, which, though late, will not fail to come.

Social Destiny of Man: or Association and Reorganization of Industry. By ALBERT BRISBANE. Philadelphia. 12mo, pp. 480.

This work is designed to give a condensed view of the system of M. Fourier, for the improvement and elevation of productive industry. It will be read with deep interest by a large class of our population. The name of Fourier may be placed at the head of modern thinkers, whose attention has been given to the practical evils of society and the means of their removal. His general principles should be cautiously separated from the details which accompany their exposition, many of which are so exclusively adapted to the French character, as to prejudice their reception with persons of opposite habits and associations. The great question, which he brings up for discussion, concerns the union of labor and capital in the same individuals, by a system of combined and organized industry. This question, it is more than probable, will not be set aside at once, whenever its importance is fully perceived, and those who are interested in its decision will find materials of no small value in the writings of M. Fourier. They may be regarded, in some sense, as the scientific analysis of the coöperative principle, which has, within a few years past, engaged the public attention in England, and in certain cases, received a successful, practical application.

Michael Angelo, considered as a Philosophic Poet, with Translations. By JOHN EDWARD TAYLOR. London: Saunders & Otley, Conduit Street. 1840.

We welcome this little book with joy, and a hope that it may be republished in Boston. It would find, probably, but a small circle of readers, but that circle would be more ready to receive and prize it than the English public, for whom it was intended, if we may judge by the way in which Mr. Taylor, all through his prefatory essay, has considered it necessary to apologize for, or, at least, explain views very commonly received among ourselves.

The essay is interesting from the degree of acquaintance it exhibits with some of those great ones, who have held up the highest aims to the soul, and from the degree of insight which reverence and delicacy of mind have given to the author. From every line comes the soft breath of green pastures where "walk the good shepherds."

Of the sonnets, we doubt the possibility of making good translations into English. No gift of the Muse is more injured by change of form than the Italian sonnet. As those of Petrarch will not bear it, from their infinite grace, those of Dante from their mystic and subtle majesty; so these of Angelo, from the rugged naiveté with which they are struck off from the mind, as huge splinters of stone might be from some vast block, can never be "done into English," as the old translators, with an intelligent modesty, were wont to write of their work. The grand thought is not quite evaporated in the process, but the image of the stern and stately writer is lost. We do not know again such words as "concetto," "superna" in their English representatives.

But since a knowledge of the Italian language is not so common an attainment as could be wished, we ought to be grateful for this attempt to extend the benefit of these noble expressions of the faith which inspired one of the most full and noble lives that has ever redeemed and encouraged man.

Fidelity must be the highest merit of these translations; for not even an Angelo could translate his peer. This, so far as we have looked at them, they seem to possess. And even in the English dress, we think none, to whom they are new, can read the sonnets, —

> "Veggio nel volto tuo col pensier mie."
> "S'un casto amor, s'una pietà superna."
> "La vita del mio amor non è cuor mio."

and others of the same pure religion, without a delight which shall

> "Cast a light upon the day,
> A light which will not go away,
> A sweet forewarning."

We hope they may have the opportunity. It is a very little book with a great deal in it, and five hundred copies will sell in two years.

We add Mr. Taylor's little preface, which happily expresses his design.

"The remarks on the poetry and philosophy of Michael Angelo, which are prefixed to these translations, have been collected and are now published, in the hope that they may invite the student of literature to trace the relation which unites the efforts of the pure intelligence and the desires of the heart to their highest earthly accomplishment under the complete forms of Art. For the example of so eminent a mind, watched and judged not only by its finished works, but, as it were, in its growth and from its inner source of Love and Knowledge, cannot but enlarge the range of our sympathy for the best powers and productions of man. And if these pages should meet with any readers inclined, like their writer, to seek and to admire the veiled truth and solemn beauty of the elder time, they will add their humble testimony to the fact, that whatever be the purpose and tendencies of the time we live in, we are not all unmindful of the better part of our inheritance in this world."

The Worship of the Soul. A Discourse preached to the Third Congregational Society in Chelsea, at the Dedication of their Chapel, on Sunday Morning, September 13, 1840. By SAMUEL D. ROBBINS. Chelsea and Boston: B. H. Greene. 1840. 8vo, pp. 16.

This Discourse is pervaded by a deeper vein of thought than we are wont to look for, or to find in the occasional services of the pulpit. We should rejoice to know that there is any considerable number of persons among the congregations that assemble in the churches for Sabbath worship, who take delight in such simple, fervent, and practical expositions of religious truth as are here set forth. This Discourse, however, indicates more than it unfolds; it is not a complete and harmonious whole; and it will be read with greater profit by those who watch for every gleam of sun-light, than by those whose eyes are open only to the broadest glare of noon.

The following passage expresses the feelings of many who are accustomed to distinguish between religion, as it existed in the divine idea of Jesus, and the religion which ventures to assume his name, as an exclusive badge at the present day.

"The occasion which assembles us is one of thrilling interest. At a day when the whole aspect of the church and the world seems to present strong tendencies toward revolution; while on all sides men seem to be outgrowing the tyranny of forms, and overleaping all former barriers which have been raised between themselves and perfect freedom, we come to consecrate this temple to the worship of the Father of our Spirits, and thus bear our humble testimony that we can find in Christian usages, and the Christian's faith, all that we need for our mental and spiritual advancement in the path to heaven. We feel, however others may consider the subject, that in the Bible and in the Saviour, are revealed to us Infinite Truths, which man can never outgrow, which as yet the world have scarcely imagined. And although we do not believe that the Christianity of Society, or the Christianity of the Church, as they appear in the present age, are by any means perfect, we do feel that the Christianity of Jesus is perfect, perpetual, and eternal: that the age will never arrive when man cannot draw from the fountain of God's truth, the waters of life and salvation." — pp. 3, 4.

The characteristics of Christianity, as described by Mr. Robbins, and the offices of the church, are worthy of attention. In reading this statement, we cannot but be struck with the incongruity between the ideal church of the preacher, and the actual church of modern society.

"I have said that Christianity is emphatically the science of the soul; and I regard this view of the religion of Jesus as infinitely important. We have our Universities and our Schools which are instituted for the purpose of teaching and explaining the natural sciences and the philosophy of the intellect. But the Church is consecrated only to the higher purposes of instruction in the knowledge of the human heart and conscience; in the mysteries of the soul, its laws and duties and destiny. We gather ourselves into this holy place to learn those mighty truths which relate to God and man. We come up hither from the world and its trials and dangers to listen to the wisdom of Jesus, and learn those deep lessons of faith and obedience and love, by which we are to become ripened daily into the image of Infinite Holiness.

"There is a higher life than that which most spirits live. A higher love than most spirits know. There is an infinity in the human soul which few have yet believed, and after which few have aspired. There is a lofty power of moral principle in the depths of our nature, which is nearly allied to omnipotence; compared with which the whole force of outward nature is more feeble than an infant's grasp. There is a might within the soul which sets at nought all outward things; and there is a joy unspeakable and full of glory, dwelling in the recesses of the good man's heart too vast for utterance. There is a spiritual insight to which the pure soul reaches, more clear and prophetic, more wide and vast than all telescopic vision can typify. There is a faith in God and a clear perception of his will and designs and Providence and Glory, which gives to its possessor a confidence and patience and sweet composure, under every varied and troublous aspect of events, such as no man can realize, who has not felt its influences in his own heart. There is a communion with God in which the soul feels the presence of the unseen One, in the profound depths of its being, with a vivid distinctness, and a holy reverence, such as no word can describe. There is a state of union of spirit with God, I do not say often reached, yet it has been attained in this world, in which all the past and present, and future seem reconciled, and Eternity is won and enjoyed; and God and man, earth and heaven with all their mysteries are apprehended in truth, as they lie in the mind of the Infinite. But the struggle with most beings is to spiritualize the actual, to make those things which are immediately around them subserve the higher interests of their immortal nature; and finding that it is almost impossible to do this, they faint in the way, and postpone to a future life that higher being which their thought apprehends, and their hearts long for, but cannot reach. Hence it is that the advanced powers of the soul of which I have been speaking are not believed to exist for us, in this world at least; and therefore the few who will strive for them, because they dare not compromise their highest thought and life and love, are looked upon as spiritual star-gazers, as visionaries dwelling amid the beautiful creations of their own ardent hearts. Hence it is that in our age the Church and its highest influences is needed, to declare to the wide world those precious promises which are destined to carry comfort and peace to the deepest emotions of the struggling soul; to speak to all men everywhere in the name of Jesus, teaching them that the highest and loveliest visions which the human mind in its most rapt hour of aspiration, has enjoyed of Truth and Life, of Holiness and Love of duty and denial of growth and glory of Faith and God, are only the faintest sketches of that reality which Christianity has brought to light." — pp. 9-11.

Essays and Poems. By JONES VERY. Boston: C. C. Little and James Brown

This little volume would have received an earlier notice, if we had been at all careful to proclaim our favorite books. The genius of this book is religious, and reaches an extraordinary depth of sentiment. The author, plainly a man of a pure and kindly temper, casts himself into the state of the high and transcendental obedience to the inward Spirit. He has apparently made up his mind to follow all its leadings, though he should be taxed with absurdity or even with insanity. In this enthusiasm he writes most of these verses, which rather flow through him than from him. There is no *composition,* no elaboration, no artifice in the structure of the rhyme, no variety in the imagery; in short, no pretension to literary merit, for this would be departure from his singleness, and followed by loss of insight. He is not at liberty even to correct these unpremeditated poems for the press; but if another will publish them, he offers no objection. In this way they have come into the world, and as yet have hardly begun to be known. With the exception of the few first poems, which appear to be of an earlier date, all these verses bear the unquestionable stamp of grandeur. They are the breathings of a certain entranced devotion, which one would say, should be received with affectionate and sympathizing curiosity by all men, as if no recent writer had so much to show them of what is most their own. They are as sincere a litany as the Hebrew songs of David or Isaiah, and only less than they, because indebted to the Hebrew muse for their tone and genius. This makes the singularity of the book, namely, that so pure an utterance of the most domestic and primitive of all sentiments should in this age of revolt and experiment use once more the popular religious language, and so show itself secondary and morbid. These sonnets have little range of topics, no extent of observation, no playfulness; there is even a certain torpidity in the concluding lines of some of them, which reminds one of church hymns; but, whilst they flow with great sweetness, they have the sublime unity of the Decalogue or the Code of Menu, and if as monotonous, yet are they almost as pure as the sounds of surrounding Nature. We gladly insert from a newspaper the following sonnet, which appeared since the volume was printed.

THE BARBERRY BUSH

The bush that has most briars and bitter fruit,
Wait till the frost has turned its green leaves red,
Its sweetened berries will thy palate suit,
And thou may'st find e'en there a homely bread.
Upon the hills of Salem scattered wide,
Their yellow blossoms gain the eye in Spring;
And straggling e'en upon the turnpike's side,
Their ripened branches to your hand they bring,
I've plucked them oft in boyhood's early hour,
That then I gave such name, and thought it true;
But now I know that other fruit as sour
Grows on what now thou callest *Me* and *You;*
Yet, wilt thou wait the autumn that I see,
Will sweeter taste than these red berries be.

At the request of a friend the following notice is inserted of a book about to be published, called "The Ideal Man." Boston: E. P. Peabody. 1842.

This book is somewhat out of the common course of American books on manners, morals, and religion. But we think it had better have been named the Cultivated Gentleman, than to have assumed the title of *The Ideal Man.* It is a manual of good manners, of pure aims, and of honorable and praiseworthy conduct, and especially is opposed to that negligence of form which runs so to excess with us. But it does not recommend or tolerate anything hollow or unmeaning. The good manners must signify good taste, good morals, good learning, and sincere religion. It bears marks of being written by a foreigner, in its style as well as matter, though he writes in the character of an American.

The Zincali: or an Account of the Gypsies of Spain; with an Original Collection of their Songs and Poetry. By George Borrow. Two Volumes in New York: Wiley & Putnam.

Our list of tribes in America indigenous and imported wants the Gypsies, as the Flora of the western hemisphere wants the race of heaths. But as it is all one to the urchin of six years, whether the fine toys are to be found in his father's house or across the road at his grandfather's, so we have always domesticated the Gypsy in school-boy literature from the English tales and traditions. This reprinted London book is equally sure of being read here as in England, and is a most acceptable gift to the lovers of the wild and wonderful. There are twenty or thirty pages in it of fascinating romantic attraction, and the whole book, though somewhat rudely and miscellaneously put together, is animated, and tells us what we wish to know. Mr. Borrow visited the Gypsies in Spain and elsewhere, as an agent of the British and Foreign Bible Society, and seems to have been commended to this employment by the rare accomplishment of a good acquaintance with the language of this singular people. How he acquired his knowledge of their speech, which seems to have opened their hearts to him, he does not inform us; and he appears to have prospered very indifferently in the religious objects of his mission; but to have really had that in his nature or education which gave him access to the Gypsy gang, so that he has seen them, talked confidentially with them, and brought away something distinct enough from them.

He has given us sketches of their past and present manner of life and employments, in the different European states, collected a strange little magazine of their poetry, and added a vocabulary of their language. He has interspersed some anecdotes of life and manners, which are told with great spirit.

This book is very entertaining, and yet, out of mere love and respect to human nature, we must add that this account of the Gypsy race must be imperfect and very partial, and that the author never sees his object quite near enough. For, on the whole, the impression made by the book is dismal; the poverty, the employments, conversations, mutual behavior of the Gypsies, are dismal; the poetry is dismal. Men do not love to be dismal, and always have their own reliefs. If we take Mr. Borrow's story as final, here is a great people subsisting for centuries unmixed with the surrounding population, like a bare and blasted heath in the midst of smiling plenty, yet cherishing their wretchedness, by rigorous usage and tradition, as if they loved it. It is an aristocracy of rags, and suffering, and vice, yet as exclusive as the patricians of wealth and power. We infer that the picture is false; that resources and compensations exist, which are not shown us. If Gypsies are pricked, we believe they will bleed; if wretched, they will jump at the first opportunity of bettering their condition. What unmakes man is essentially incredible. The air may be loaded with fogs or with fetid gases, and continue respirable; but if it be decomposed, it can no longer sustain life. The condition of the Gypsy may be bad enough, tried by the scale of English comfort, and yet appear tolerable and pleasant to the Gypsy, who finds attractions in his out-door way of living, his freedom, and sociability, which the Agent of the Bible Society does not reckon. And we think that a traveller of another way of thinking would not find the Gypsy so void of conscience as Mr. Borrow paints him, as the differences in that particular are universally exaggerated in daily conversation. And lastly, we suspect the walls of separation between the Gypsy and the surrounding population are less firm than we are here given to understand.

Ancient Spanish Ballads, Historical and Romantic. Translated, with Notes. By J. G. LOCKHART. New York: Wiley & Putnam.

The enterprising publishers, Messrs. Wiley & Putnam, who have reprinted, in a plain but very neat form, Mr. Lockhart's gorgeously illustrated work, have judiciously prefixed to it, by way of introduction, a critique on the book from the Edinburgh Review, and have added at the end of the volume an analytical account, with specimens of the Romance of the Cid, from the Penny Magazine. This is done with the greatest propriety, for the Cid seems to be the proper centre of Spanish legendary poetry. The Iliad, the Nibelungen, the Cid, the Robin Hood Ballads, Frithiof's Saga, (for the last also depends for its merit on its fidelity to the legend,) are five admirable collections of early popular poetry of so many nations; and with whatever difference of form, they possess strong mutual resemblances, chiefly apparent in the spirit which they communicate to the reader, of health, vigor, cheerfulness, and good hope. In this day of reprinting and of restoration, we hope that Southey's Chronicle of the Cid, which is a kind of "Harmony of the Gospels" of the Spanish Romance, may be republished in a volume of convenient size. That is a strong book, and makes lovers and admirers of "My Cid, the Perfect one, who was born in a fortunate hour." Its traits of heroism and bursts of simple emotion, once read, can never be forgotten; "I am not a man to be besieged;" and "God! What a glad man was the Cid on that day," and many the like words still ring in our ears. The Cortes at Toledo, where judgment was given between the Cid and his sons-in-law, is one of the strongest dramatic scenes in literature. Several of the best ballads in Mr. Lockhart's collection recite incidents of the Cid's history. The best ballad in the book is the "Count Alarcos and the Infanta Solisa," which is a meet companion for Chaucer's Griselda. The "Count Garci Perez de Vargas" is one of our favorites; and there is one called the "Bridal of Andalla," which we have long lost all power to read as a poem, since we have heard it sung by a voice so rich, and sweet, and penetrating, as to make the ballad the inalienable property of the singer.

Tecumseh; a Poem. By GEORGE H. COLTON. New York: Wiley & Putnam

This pleasing summer-day story is the work of a well read, cultivated writer, with a skilful ear, and an evident admirer of Scott and Campbell. There is a metrical sweetness and calm perception of beauty spread over the poem, which declare that the poet enjoyed his own work; and the smoothness and literary finish of the cantos seem to indicate more years than it appears our author has numbered. Yet the perusal suggested that the author had written this poem in the feeling, that the delight he has experienced from Scott's effective lists of names might be reproduced in America by the enumeration of the sweet and sonorous Indian names of our waters. The success is exactly correspondent. The verses are tuneful, but are secondary; and remind the ear so much of the model, as to show that the noble aboriginal names were not suffered to make their own measures in the poet's ear, but must modulate their wild beauty to a foreign metre. They deserved better at the author's hands. We felt, also, the objection that is apt to lie against poems on new subjects by persons versed in old books, that the costume is exaggerated at the expense of the man. The most Indian thing about the Indian is surely not his moccasins, or his calumet, his wampum, or his stone hatchet, but traits of character and sagacity, skill or passion; which would be intelligible at Paris or at Pekin, and which Scipio or Sidney, Lord Clive or Colonel Crockett would be as likely to exhibit as Osceola and Black Hawk.

Poems. By ALFRED TENNYSON. Two Volumes. Boston: W. D. Ticknor

Tennyson is more simply the songster than any poet of our time. With him the delight of musical expression is first, the thought second. It was well observed by one of our companions, that he has described just what we should suppose to be his method of composition in this verse from "The Miller's Daughter."

"A love-song I had somewhere read,
An echo from a measured strain,
Beat time to nothing in my head
From some odd corner of the brain.
It haunted me, the morning long,
With weary sameness in the rhymes,
The phantom of a silent song,
That went and came a thousand times."

So large a proportion of even the good poetry of our time is either over-ethical or over-passionate, and the stock poetry is so deeply tainted with a sentimental egotism, that this, whose chief merits lay in its melody and picturesque power, was most refreshing. What a relief, after sermonizing and wailing had dulled the sense with such a weight of cold abstraction, to be soothed by this ivory lute!

Not that he wanted nobleness and individuality in his thoughts, or a due sense of the poet's vocation; but he won us to truths, not forced them upon us; as we listened, the cope

> "Of the self-attained futurity
> Was cloven with the million stars which tremble
> O'er the deep mind of dauntless infamy."

And he seemed worthy thus to address his friend,

> "Weak truth a-leaning on her crutch,
> Wan, wasted truth in her utmost need,
> Thy kingly intellect shall feed,
> Until she be an athlete bold."

Unless thus sustained, the luxurious sweetness of his verse must have wearied. Yet it was not of aim or meaning we thought most, but of his exquisite sense for sounds and melodies, as marked by himself in the description of Cleopatra.

> "Her warbling voice, a lyre of widest range,
> Touched by all passion, did fall down and glance
> From tone to tone, and glided through all change
> Of liveliest utterance."

Or in the fine passage in the Vision of Sin, where

> "Then the music touched the gates and died;
> Rose again from where it seemed to fail,
> Stormed in orbs of song, a growing gale;" &c.

Or where the Talking Oak composes its serenade for the pretty Alice; — but indeed his descriptions of melody are almost as abundant as his melodies, though the central music of the poet's mind is, he says, as that of the

> "fountain
> Like sheet lightning,
> Ever brightening
> With a low melodious thunder;
> All day and all night it is ever drawn
> From the brain of the purple mountain
> Which stands in the distance yonder:
> It springs on a level of bowery lawn,
> And the mountain draws it from heaven above,
> And it sings a song of undying love."

Next to his music, his delicate, various, gorgeous music, stands his power of picturesque representation. And his, unlike those of most poets, are eye-pictures, not mind-pictures. And yet there is no hard or tame fidelity, but a simplicity and ease at representation (which is quite another thing from reproduction) rarely to be paralleled. How, in the Palace of Art, for instance, they are unrolled slowly and gracefully, as if painted one after another on the same canvass. The touch is calm and masterly, though the result is looked at with a sweet, self-pleasing eye. Who can forget such as this, and of such there are many, painted with as few strokes and with as complete a success?

> "A still salt pool, locked in with bars of sand;
> Left on the shore; that hears all night
> The plunging seas draw backward from the land
> Their moon-led waters white."

Tennyson delights in a garden. Its groups, and walks, and mingled bloom intoxicate him, and us through him. So high is his organization, and so powerfully stimulated by color and perfume, that it heightens all our senses too, and the rose is glorious, not from detecting its ideal beauty, but from a perfection of hue and scent, we never felt before. All the earlier poems are flower-like, and this tendency is so strong in him, that a friend observed, he could not keep up the character of the tree in his Oak of Summer Chase, but made it talk like an "enormous flower." The song,

> "A spirit haunts the year's last hours,"

is not to be surpassed for its picture of the autumnal garden.

The new poems, found in the present edition, show us our friend of ten years since much altered, yet the same. The light he sheds on the world is mellowed and tempered. If the charm he threw around us before was somewhat too sensuous, it is not so now; he is deeply thoughtful; the dignified and graceful man has displaced the Antinous beauty of the youth. His melody is less rich, less intoxicating, but deeper; a sweetness from the soul, sweetness as of the hived honey of fine experiences, replaces the sweetness which captivated the ear only, in many of his earlier verses. His range of subjects was great before, and is now such that he would seem too merely the amateur, but for the success in each, which says that the same fluent and apprehensive nature, which threw itself with such ease into the forms of outward beauty, has now been intent rather on the secrets of the shaping spirit. In "Locksley Hall," "St. Simeon Stylites," "Ulysses," "Love and Duty," "The Two Voices," are deep tones, that bespeak that acquaintance with realities, of which, in the "Palace of Art," he had expressed his need. The keen sense of outward beauty, the ready shaping fancy, had not been suffered to degrade the poet into that basest of beings, an intellectual voluptuary, and a pensive but serene wisdom hallows all his song.

His opinions on subjects, that now divide the world, are stated in two or three of these pieces, with that temperance and candor of thought, now more rare even than usual, and with a simplicity bordering on homeliness of diction, which is peculiarly pleasing, from the sense of plastic power and refined good sense it imparts.

A gentle and gradual style of narration, without prolixity or tameness, is seldom to be found in the degree in which such pieces as "Dora" and "Godiva" display it. The grace of the light ballad pieces is as remarkable in its way, as was his grasp and force in "Oriana." "The Lord of Burleigh," "Edward Gray," and "Lady Clare," are distinguished for different shades of this light grace, tender, and speaking more to the soul than the sense, like the different hues in the landscape, when the sun is hid in clouds, so gently shaded that they seem but the echoes of themselves.

I know not whether most to admire the bursts of passion in "Locksley Hall," the playful sweetness of the "Talking Oak," or the mere catching of a cadence in such slight things as

> "Break, break, break
> On thy cold gray stones, O sea," &c.

Nothing is more uncommon than the lightness of touch, which gives a charm to such little pieces as the "Skipping Rope."

We regret much to miss from this edition "The Mystic," "The Deserted House," and "Elegiacs," all favorites for years past, and not to be disparaged in favor of any in the present collection. England, we believe, has not shown a due sense of the merits of this poet, and to us is given the honor of rendering homage more readily to an accurate and elegant intellect, a musical reception of nature, a high tendency in thought, and a talent of singular fineness, flexibility, and scope.

A Letter to Rev. Wm. E. Channing, D.D. By O. A. Brownson. Boston: Charles C. Little and James Brown. 1842.

That there is no knowledge of God possible to man but a subjective knowledge, — no revelation but the development of the individual within himself, and to himself, — are prevalent statements, which Mr. Brownson opposes by a single formula, that *life is relative in its very nature.* God alone is; all creatures live by virtue of what is not themselves, no less than by virtue of what is themselves, the prerogative of man being to do consciously, that is, more or less, intelligently. Mr. Brownson carefully discriminates between Essence and Life. Essence, being object to itself, alone has freedom, which is what the old theologians named sovereignty; — a noble word for the thing intended, were it not desecrated in our associations, in being usurped by creatures that are slaves to time and circumstance. But life implies a causative object, as well as causative subject; wherefore *creatures* are only free by Grace of God.

That men should live, with God for predominating object, is the Ideal of Humanity, or the Law of Holiness, in the highest sense; for this object alone can emancipate them from what is below themselves.

But a nice discrimination must be made here. The Ideal of Humanity, as used by Mr. Brownson, does not mean the highest idea of himself, which a man can form by induction on himself as an individual; it means God's idea of man, which shines into every man from the beginning; " Enlighteneth every man that cometh into the world," though his darkness comprehendeth it not, until it is " made flesh." It is by virtue of that freedom which is God's alone, and which is the issue of absolute love, that is, " because God so loved the world," he takes up the subject, Jesus, and makes himself objective to him without measure, thereby rendering his life as divine as it is human, though it remains also as human, — strictly speaking, — as it is divine.

To all men's consciousness it is true that God is objective in a degree, or they were not distinctively human. His glory is refracted, as it were, to their eyes, through the universe. But only in a man, to whom he has made himself the imperative object, does he approach men, in all points, in such degree as to make them divine. He is no less free (sovereign) in coming to each man in Christ, than, in the first instance, in making Jesus of Nazareth the Christ. Men are only free inasmuch as they are open to this majestic access, and are able to pray with St. Augustine, " What art thou to me, oh Lord? *Have mercy on me that I may ask.* The house of my soul is too strait for thee to come into; but let it, oh Lord, be enlarged by thee. It is ruinous, but let it be repaired by thee," &c.

The Unitarian Church, as Mr. Brownson thinks, indicates truth, in so far as it insists on the life of Jesus as being that wherein we find grace; but in so far as it does not perceive that this life is something more than a series of good actions, which others may reproduce, it leans on an arm of flesh, and puts an idol in the place of Christ. The Trinitarian Church, he thinks, therefore, has come nearer the truth, by its formulas of doctrine; and especially the Roman Catholic Church, by the Eucharist. The error of both Churches has been to predicate of the being, Jesus, what is only true of his life. The being, Jesus, was a man; his life is God. It is the doctrine of John the Evangelist throughout, that the soul lives by the real presence of Jesus Christ, as literally as the body lives by bread. The unchristianized live only partially, by so much of the word as shines in the darkness which may not hinder it quite. This partial life repeats in all time the prophecies of antiquity, and is another witness to Jesus Christ, "the same yesterday, to-day, and forever."

Mr. Brownson thinks that he has thus discovered a formula of "the faith once delivered to the saints," which goes behind and annihilates the controversy between Unitarians and Trinitarians, and may lead them both to a deeper comprehension and clearer expression of the secret of life.

Confessions of St. Augustine. Boston: E. P. Peabody

We heartily welcome this reprint from the recent London edition, which was a revision, by the Oxford divines, of an old English translation. It is a rare addition to our religious library. The great Augustine, — one of the truest, richest, subtlest, eloquentest of authors, comes now in this American dress, to stand on the same shelf with his far-famed disciples, with A-Kempis, Herbert, Taylor, Scougal, and Fenelon. The Confessions have also a high interest as one of the honestest autobiographies ever written. In this view it takes even rank with Montaigne's Essays, with Luther's Table Talk, the Life of John Bunyan, with Rousseau's Confessions, and the Life of Dr. Franklin. In opening the book at random, we have fallen on his reflections on the death of his early friend.

"O madness, which knowest not how to love men like men! I fretted, sighed, wept, was distracted, had neither rest nor counsel. For I bore about a shattered and bleeding soul, impatient of being borne by me, yet where to repose it I found not. All things looked ghastly; yea, the very light; whatsoever was not what he was, was revolting and hateful, except groaning and tears. In those alone found I a little refreshment. I fled out of my country; for so should mine eyes look less for him where they were not wont to see him. And thus from Thagaste I came to Carthage. Times lose no time; nor do they roll idly by; through our senses they work strange operations on the mind. Behold, they went and came day by day, and by coming and going introduced into my mind other imaginations and other remembrances; and little by little patched me up again with my old kind of delights unto which that my sorrow gave way. And yet there succeeded not indeed other griefs, yet the causes of other griefs. For whence had that former grief so easily reached my inmost soul but that I had poured out my soul upon the dust in loving one, that must die, as if he would never die. For what restored and refreshed me chiefly, was the solaces of other friends with whom I did love what instead of thee I loved: and this was a great fable and protracted lie, by whose adulterous stimulus our soul, which lay itching in our ears, was defiled. But that fable would not die to me so oft as any of my friends died. There were other things which in them did more take my mind; to talk and jest together; to do kind offices by turns; to read together honied books; to play the fool or be earnest together; to dissent at times without discontent, as a man might with his ownself; and even with the seldomness of those dissentings, to season our more frequent consentings; sometimes to teach, and sometimes learn; long for the absent with impatience, and welcome the coming with joy."

The Bible in Spain, or the Journeys, Adventures, and Imprisonments of an Englishman in an attempt to circulate the Scriptures in the Peninsula. By GEORGE BORROW. Author of "The Gypsies in Spain."

This is a charming book, full of free breezes, and mountain torrents, and pictures of romantic interest. Mr. Borrow is a self-sufficing man of free nature, his mind is always in the fresh air; he is not unworthy to climb the sierras and rest beneath the cork trees where we have so often enjoyed the company of Don Quixote. And he has the merit, almost miraculous to-day, of leaving us almost always to draw our own inferences from what he gives us. We can wander on in peace, secure against being forced back upon ourselves, or forced sideways to himself. It is as good to read through this book of pictures, as to stay in a house hung with Gobelin tapestry. The Gypsies are introduced here with even more spirit than in his other book. He sketches men and nature with the same bold and clear, though careless touch. Cape Finisterre and the entrance into Gallicia are as good parts as any to look at.

Paracelsus

Mr. Browning was known to us before, by a little book called "Pippa Passes," full of bold openings, motley with talent like this, and rich in touches of personal experience. A version of the thought of the day so much less penetrating than Faust and Festus cannot detain us long; yet we are pleased to see each man in his kind bearing witness, that neither sight nor thought will enable to attain that golden crown which is the reward of life, of profound experiences and gradual processes, the golden crown of wisdom. The artist nature is painted with great vigor in Aprile. The author has come nearer that, than to the philosophic nature. There is music in the love of Festus for his friend, especially in the last scene, the thought of his taking sides with him against the divine judgment is true as poesy.

Antislavery Poems. By JOHN PIERPONT. Boston: Oliver Johnson. 1843

These poems are much the most readable of all the metrical pieces we have met with on the subject; indeed, it is strange how little poetry this old outrage of negro slavery has produced. Cowper's lines in the Task are still the best we have. Mr. Pierpont has a good deal of talent, and writes very spirited verses, full of point. He has no continuous meaning which enables him to write a long and equal poem, but every poem is a series of detached epigrams, some better, some worse. His taste is not always correct, and from the boldest flight he shall suddenly alight in very low places. Neither is the motive of the poem ever very high, so that they seem to be rather squibs than prophecies or imprecations; but for political satire, we think the "Word from a Petitioner" very strong, and the "Gag" the best piece of poetical indignation in America.

Sonnets and other Poems. By WILLIAM LLOYD GARRISON. Boston. 1843. pp. 96

Mr. Garrison has won his palms in quite other fields than those of the lyric muse, and he is far more likely to be the subject than the author of good poems. He is rich enough in the earnestness and the success of his character to be patient with the very rapid withering of the poetic garlands he has snatched in passing. Yet though this volume contains little poetry, both the subjects and the sentiments will everywhere command respect. That piece in the volume, which pleased us most, was the address to his first-born child.

America — an Ode; and other Poems. By N. W. COFFIN. Boston: S. G. Simpkins

Our Mæcenas shakes his head very doubtfully at this well-printed Ode, and only says, "An ode nowadays needs to be admirable to carry sail at all. Mr. Sprague's Centennial Ode, and Ode at the Shakspeare Jubilee, are the only American lyrics that we have prospered in reading, — if we dare still remember them." Yet he adds mercifully, "The good verses run like golden brooks through the dark forests of toil, rippling and musical, and undermine the heavy banks till they fall in and are borne away. Thirty-five pieces follow the Ode, of which everything is neat, pretty, harmonious, tasteful, the sentiment pleasing, manful, if not inspired. If the poet have nothing else, he has a good ear."

Poems by WILLIAM ELLERY CHANNING. Boston. 1843

We have already expressed our faith in Mr. Channing's genius, which in some of the finest and rarest traits of the poet is without a rival in this country. This little volume has already become a sign of great hope and encouragement to the lovers of the muse. The refinement and the sincerity of his mind, not less than the originality and delicacy of the diction, are not merits to be suddenly apprehended, but are sure to find a cordial appreciation. Yet we would willingly invite any lover of poetry to read "The Earth-Spirit," "Reverence," "The Lover's Song," "Death," and "The Poet's Hope."

To Correspondents

We are greatly indebted to several friends, for the most part anonymous, for literary contributions, and not less indebted in those cases in which we have not found the pieces sufficiently adapted to our purpose to print them. The Dial has been almost as much a journal of friendship as of literature and morals, and its editors have felt the offer of any literary aid as a token of personal kindness. Had it been practicable, we should gladly have obeyed the wish to make a special acknowledgment of each paper that has been confided to us, explaining in each instance the reason for withholding it. We wish to say to our Correspondents, that, printed or unprinted, these papers are welcome and useful to us, if only as they confirm or qualify our own opinions, and give us insight into the thinking of others.

In the last quarter, we have received several papers, some of which, after some hesitation, we decide not to print. One of these is a translation which (without comparing it with the original) seems to us excellent, of Schiller's Critique on Goethe's Egmont, and that it may not through our omission, fail to be read, we shall leave the MS. for a time with our publishers, subject to the order of the writer. We have also received from A. Z. a poetical translation from Richter; from A. C. L. A. a paper on the Spirit of Polytheism; from a friend at Byfield, a poetical fragment called "The Ship;" from our correspondent C. at New Bedford, a poem called "The Two Argosies;" from R. P. R. some elegiac verses; from J. A. S. "Lady Mirbel's Dirge."

The Huguenots in France and America

The Huguenots is a very entertaining book, drawn from excellent sources, rich in its topics, describing many admirable persons and events, and supplies an old defect in our popular literature. The editor's part is performed with great assiduity and conscience. Yet amidst this enumeration of all the geniuses, and beauties, and sanctities of France, what has the greatest man in France, at that period, Michael de Montaigne, done, or left undone, that his name should be quite omitted?

The Spanish Student. A Play in Three Acts. By H. W. Longfellow

A pleasing tale, but Cervantes shall speak for us out of *La Gitanilla.*

"You must know, Preciosa, that as to this name of *Poet,* few are they who deserve it, — and I am no *Poet,* but only a lover of Poesy, so that I have no need to beg or borrow the verses of others. The verses, I gave you the other day, are mine, and those of to-day as well; — but, for all that, I am no poet, neither is it my prayer to be so."

"Is it then so bad a thing to be a poet?" asked Preciosa.

"Not bad," replied the Page, "but to be a poet and nought else, I do not hold to be very good. For poetry should be like a precious jewel, whose owner does not put it on every day, nor show it to the world at every step; but only when it is fitting, and when there is a reason for showing it. Poetry is a most lovely damsel; chaste, modest, and discreet; spirited, but yet retiring, and ever holding itself within the strictest rule of honor. She is the friend of Solitude. She finds in the fountains her delight, in the fields her counsellor, in the trees and flowers enjoyment and repose; and lastly, she charms and instructs all that approach her."

The Dream of a Day, and other Poems. By JAMES G. PERCIVAL. New Haven, 1843

Mr. Percival printed his last book of poems sixteen years ago, and every school-boy learned to declaim his "Bunker Hill," since which time, he informs us, his studies have been for the most part very adverse to poetic inspirations. Yet here we have specimens of no less than one hundred and fifty different forms of stanza. Such thorough workmanship in the poetical art is without example or approach in this country, and deserves all honor. We have imitations of four of the leading classes of ancient measures, — the Dactylic, Iambic, Anapestic, and Trochaic, to say nothing of rarer measures, now never known out of colleges. Then come songs for national airs, formed on the rhythm of the music, including

Norwegian, German, Russian, Bohemian, Gaelic, and Welsh, — Teutonian and Slavonian. But unhappily this diligence is not without its dangers. It has prejudiced the creative power,

> " And made that art, which was a rage."

Neatness, terseness, objectivity, or at any rate the absence of subjectivity, characterize these poems. Our bard has not quite so much fire as we had looked for, grows warm but does not ignite; those sixteen years of " adverse " studies have had their effect on Pegasus, who now trots soundly and resolutely on, but forbears rash motions, and never runs away with us. The old critics of England were hardly steadier to their triad of " Gower, Lydgate, and Chaucer," than our American magazines to the trinity of " Bryant, Dana, and Percival." A gentle constellation truly, all of the established religion, having the good of their country and their species at heart. Percival has not written anything quite as good on the whole as his two fast associates, but surpasses them both in labor, in his mimetic skill, and in his objectiveness. He is the most objective of the American Poets. Bryant has a superb propriety of feeling, has plainly always been in good society, but his sweet oaten pipe discourses only pastoral music. Dana has the most established religion, more sentiment, more reverence, more of England; whilst Mr. Percival is an upright, soldierly, free-spoken man, very much of a patriot, hates cant, and does his best.

POEMS

POEMS

MY THOUGHTS

Many are the thoughts that come to me
  In my lonely musings;
And they drift so strange and swift,
  There's no time for choosing
Which to follow, for to leave
  Any, seems a loosing.

When they come, they come in flocks,
  As on glancing feather,
Startled birds rise one by one
  In Autumnal weather,
Waking one another up
  From the sheltering heather.

Some so merry that I laugh,
  Some so grave and serious,
Some so trite, their least approach
  Is enough to weary us: —

Others flit like midnight ghosts,
Shrouded and mysterious.

There are thoughts that o'er me steal,
Like the day when dawning;
Great thoughts winged with melody
Common utterance scorning,
Moving in an inward tune,
And an inward morning.

Some have dark and drooping wings,
Children all of sorrow;
Some are as gay, as if to-day
Could see no cloudy morrow, —
And yet, like light and shade, they each
Must from the other borrow.

One by one they come to me
On their destined mission;
One by one I see them fade
With no hopeless vision;
For they've led me on a step
To their home Elysian.

THE PHOENIX.[1]

My bosom's Phoenix has assured
His nest in sky-vault's cope,
In the body's eye immured
He is weary of life's hope.

Round and round this heap of ashes
Now flies the bird amain,
But in that odorous niche of heaven
Nestles the bird again.

[1] The Soul.

Once flies he upward, he will perch
  On Tuba's[1] golden bough;
His home is on that fruited arch
  Which cools the blest below.

If over this world of ours
  His wings my Phoenix spread,
How gracious falls on land and sea
  The soul-refreshing shade!

Either world inhabits he,
  Sees oft below him planets roll;
His body is all of air compact,
  Of Allah's love, his soul.

FAITH

PLUNGE in your angry waves,
  Defying doubt and care,
And the flowing of the seven broad seas
  Shall never wet thy hair.

Is Allah's face on thee
  Bending with love benign?
Thou too on Allah's countenance
  O fairest! turnest thine.

And though thy fortune and thy form
  Be broken, waste and void,
Though suns be spent, of thy life-root
  No fibre is destroyed.

[1] The Tree of Life.

THE POET

HOARD knowledge in thy coffers,
  The lightest load to bear;
Ingots of gold, and diamonds,
  Let others drag with care.

The devil's snares are strong,
  Yet have I God in need;
And if I had not God to friend,
  What can the devil speed?

Courage! Hafiz, though not thine
  Gold wedge and silver ore,
More worth to thee the gift of song,
  And the clear insight more.

I truly have no treasure,
  Yet have I rich content;
The first from Allah to the Shah,
  The last to Hafiz went.

WORD AND DEED

WHILST roses bloom along the plain,
The Nightingale to the Falcon said,
" Why of all the birds must thou be dumb?
With closed mouth thou utterest,
Though dying, no last word to man:
Yet sit'st thou on the hand of caliphs,
And feedest on the grouse's breast;
Whilst I, who hundred thousand jewels
Squander in a single tone,
Lo! I feed myself with worms,

And my dwelling is a thorn."
The Falcon answered, "Be all ear:
Thou seest I'm dumb; be thou, too, dumb.
I, experienced in affairs,
See fifty things, say never one.
But thee the people prize not,
Who, doing nothing, say a hundred.
To me, appointed to the chase,
The King's hand gives the grouse's breast,
Whilst a chatterer like thee
Must gnaw worms in the thorns. Farewell!"

TO HIMSELF

HAFIZ, speak not of thy need,
Are not these verses thine?
Then, all the poets are agreed,
Thou canst at nought repine.

LETTERS

LETTER TO CHANDLER ROBBINS

CONCORD, MARCH 2d, 1845.

MY DEAR SIR: — Had I remembered any piece of mine which seemed to have a special fitness for your purpose, I should have made an opportunity, amidst a press of petty affairs, to name it; but none occurring to me, I have left the selection to your and my good fortune. It would have given me pleasure, could I have known of the occasion earlier, and if the Muse had been willing, to have recalled for poetry, those earlier days — many anxious, many pleasant, all thoughtful days, which I spent in the service of the Second Church. I stood a few weeks ago at the foot of the new tower, and gazed up at its stately mass and proportions with great satisfaction. I hope it will confer new benefit every day as long as it shall stand.

Yours, with great regard,
RALPH WALDO EMERSON.

WILLIAM EMERSON

A LETTER TO WILLIAM B. SPRAGUE, D. D.

CONCORD, OCTOBER 5, 1849.

MY DEAR SIR:—I fear you have the worst thoughts of me as far as the virtues of a good correspondent go. I ought to have warned you at first that I am a reprobate in that matter. Yet, I did, on the receipt of your letter, in the summer, make, with my mother, some investigation into the history of my father's preaching, that he might make his own answer, as you suggested, to your inquiry concerning his opinions. But I did not find, in any manuscript or printed sermons that I looked at, any very explicit statement of opinion on the question between Calvinists and Socinians. He inclines obviously to what is ethical and universal in Christianity; very little to the personal and historical. Indeed what I found nearest approaching what would be called his creed, is in a printed Sermon "at the Ordination of Mr. Bedee, of Wilton, N. H." I think I observe in his writings, as in the writings of Unitarians down to a recent date, a studied reserve on the subject of the nature and offices of Jesus. They had not made up their own minds on it. It was a mystery to them, and they let it remain so.

Yours respectfully,
RALPH WALDO EMERSON.

LETTER TO SAMUEL GRIDLEY HOWE

ON THE NEGRO KIDNAPPING IN BOSTON

CONCORD, September 23, 1846.

DR. S. G. HOWE, AND ASSOCIATES OF THE COMMITTEE OF CITIZENS: — If I could do or say anything useful or equal to the occasion, I would not fail to attend the meeting on Thursday. I feel the irreparable shame to Boston of this abduction. I hope it is not possible that the city will make the act its own, by any color or justification. Our State has suffered many disgraces, of late years, to spoil our pride in it, but never any so flagrant as this, if the people of the Commonwealth can be brought to be accomplices in this crime, — as nothing will be too bad for their desert, — so it is very certain they will have the ignominy very faithfully put to their lips. The question you now propose, is a good test of the honesty and manliness of our commerce. If it shall turn out, as desponding men say, that our people do not really care whether Boston is a slave-port or not, provided our trade thrives, then we may, at least, cease to dread hard times and ruin. It is high time our bad wealth came to an end. I am sure, I shall very cheerfully take my share of suffering in the ruin of such a prosperity, and shall very willingly turn to the mountains to chop wood, and seek to find for myself and my children labors compatible with freedom and honor.

With this feeling, I am proportionably grateful to Mr. Adams and yourselves for undertaking the office of putting the question to our people, whether they will make this cruelty theirs? and of giving them an opportunity of clearing the population from the stain of this crime, and of securing mankind from the repetition of it, in this quarter, forever.

Respectfully and thankfully,
Your obedient servant,
RALPH WALDO EMERSON.

TWO LETTERS TO HENRY WARE, Jr.

CONCORD, July 28, 1838.

WHAT you say about the discourse at Divinity College, is just what I might expect from your truth and charity, combined with your known opinions. I am not a stock or a stone, as one said in the old time; and could not but feel pain in saying some things in that place and presence, which I supposed might meet dissent, and the dissent, I may say, of dear friends and benefactors of mine. Yet, as my conviction is perfect in the substantial truth of the doctrine of this discourse, and is not very new, you will see, at once, that it must appear to me very important that it be spoken; and I thought I would not pay the nobleness of my friends so mean a compliment, as to suppress my opposition to their supposed views out of fear of offence. I would rather say to them — These things look thus to me; to you, otherwise. Let us say out our uttermost word, and be the all-pervading truth, as it surely will, judge between us. Either of us would, I doubt not, be equally glad to be apprized of his error. Meantime, I shall be admonished by this expression of your thought, to revise with greater care the "Address" before it is printed (for the use of the class), and I heartily thank you for this renewed expression of your tried toleration and love.

Respectfully and affectionately yours,
RALPH WALDO EMERSON.

CONCORD, October 8, 1838.

MY DEAR SIR: — I ought sooner to have acknowledged your kind letter of last week, and the Sermon it accompanied. The letter was right manly and noble. The Sermon, too, I have read with attention. If it assails any doctrines of mine — perhaps I am not so quick to see it as writers generally, — certainly I did not feel any disposition to depart from my habitual contentment, that you should say your thought, whilst I say mine.

I believe I must tell you what I think of my new position. It strikes me very oddly, that good and wise men at Cambridge and Boston should think of raising me into an object of criticism. I have always been, — from my very incapacity of methodical writing, — "a chartered libertine" free to worship and free to rail, — lucky when I could make myself understood, but never esteemed near enough to the institution and mind of society to deserve the notice of the masters of literature and religion. I have appreciated fully the advantages of my position; for I well know, that there is no scholar less willing or less able to be a polemic. I could not give account of myself, if challenged. I could not possibly give you one of the "arguments" you cruelly hint at, on which any doctrine of mine stands. For I do not know what arguments mean, in reference to any expression of thought. I delight in telling what I think; but, if you ask me how I dare say so, or, why it is so, I am the most helpless of mortal men. I do not even see, that either of these questions admits of an answer. So that, in the present droll posture of my affairs, when I see myself suddenly raised into the importance of a heretic, I am very uneasy when I advert to the supposed duties of such a personage, who is to make good his thesis against all comers.

I certainly shall do no such thing. I shall read what you and other good men write, as I have always done, — glad when you speak my thoughts, and skipping the page that has nothing for me. I shall go on, just as before, seeing whatever I can, and telling what I see; and, I suppose, with the same fortune that has hitherto attended me; the joy of finding, that my abler and better brothers, who work with the sympathy of society, loving and beloved, do now and then unexpectedly confirm my perceptions, and find my nonsense is only their own thought in motley. And so I am,

Your affectionate servant,

Ralph Waldo Emerson.

LETTER TO THE SECOND CHURCH AND SOCIETY IN BOSTON

MARCH, 1829

CHRISTIAN BRETHREN AND FRIENDS: — I have received the communication transmitted to me by your committee inviting me to the office of junior pastor in your church and society. I accept the invitation. If my own feelings could have been consulted, I should have desired to postpone for at least several months my entrance into this solemn affair. I do not now approach it with any sanguine confidence in my ability nor in my prospects. I come to you in weakness and not in strength. In short, I have not yet had an abundant experience of the uncertainty of human hopes. I have learned the lesson of utter dependency, and it is in a devout reliance upon other strength than my own, in an humble trust in God to sustain me, that I put forth my hands to his great work. But, brethren, while I distrust my powers, I must speak firmly of my purpose. I well know what are the claims on your part to my best exertions, and I shall meet them, so far as in me lies, by a faithful performance of duty. I shall do all I can in approaching these duties.

I am encouraged by the strong expression of confidence and good-will I have read from you. I am encouraged by the hope of enjoying the counsel and aid of the distinguished servant of the Lord who has so long labored with you. I look to the example of the Lord in all my hopes of advancing his holy religion, and I implore the blessing of God upon this connection about to be formed between you and myself.

I am your friend and servant,

Ralph Waldo Emerson.

LETTER TO THE SECOND CHURCH AND SOCIETY

BOSTON, 22d December, 1832.

TO THE SECOND CHURCH AND SOCIETY.

CHRISTIAN FRIENDS: — Since the formal resignation of my official relation to you in my communication to the proprietors in September, I had waited anxiously for an opportunity of addressing you once more from the pulpit, though it were only to say, Let us part in peace and in the love of God. The state of my health has prevented and continues to prevent me from so doing. I am now advised to seek the benefit of a sea-voyage. I cannot go away without a brief parting word to friends who have shown me so much kindness, and to whom I have felt myself so dearly bound.

Our connection has been very short. I had only begun my work. It is now brought to a sudden close, and I look back, I own, with a painful sense of weakness, to the little service I have been able to render, after so much expectation on my part, — to the chequered space of time, which domestic affliction and personal infirmities have made yet shorter and more unprofitable.

As long as he remains in the same place, every man flatters himself, however keen may be his sense of failures and unworthiness, that he shall yet accomplish much; that the future shall make amends for the past; that his very errors shall prove his instructors, — and what limit is there to hope? But a separation from our place, the close of a particular career of duty, shuts the book, bereaves us of this hope, and leaves us only to lament how little has been done.

Yet, my friends, our faith in the great truths of the New Testament makes the change of places and circumstances, of less account to us, by fixing our attention upon that which is unalterable. I find great consolation in the thought, that the resignation of my present relations makes so little change to myself. I am no longer your minister, but am not the less engaged, I hope, to the love and service of the same eternal cause, the advancement, namely, of the kingdom of God in the hearts of men. The tie that binds each of us to that cause is not created by our connection, and can not be hurt by our separation. To me, as one disciple, is the ministry of truth, as far as I can discern and declare it, committed, and I desire to live nowhere and no longer than that grace of God is imparted to me — the liberty to seek and the liberty to utter it.

And, more than this, I rejoice to believe, my ceasing to exercise the pastoral office among you, does not make any real change in our spiritual relation to each other. Whatever is most desirable and excellent therein, remains to us. For, truly speaking, whoever provokes me to a good act or thought, has given me a pledge of his fidelity to virtue, — he has come under bonds to adhere to that cause to which we are jointly attached. And so I say to all you, who have been my counsellors and co-operators in our Christian walk, that I am wont to see in your faces, the seals and certificates of our mutual obligations. If we have conspired from week to week, in the sympathy and expression of devout sentiments; if we have received together the unspeakable gift of God's truth; if we have studied together the sense of any divine word; or striven together in any charity; or conferred together for the relief or instruction of any brother; if together we have laid down the dead in a pious hope; or held up the babe into the baptism of Christianity; above all, if we have shared in any habitual acknowledgment of that benignant God, whose omnipresence raises and glorifies the meanest offices and the lowest ability, and opens heaven in every heart that worships him, — then indeed are we united, we are mutually debtors to each other of faith and hope, engaged to persist and confirm each other's hearts in obedience to the Gospel. We shall not feel that the nominal changes and little separations of this world, can release us from the strong cordage of this spiritual bond. And I entreat you to consider how truly blessed will have been our connection, if in this manner, the memory of it shall serve to bind each one of us more strictly to the practice of our several duties. It remains to thank you for the goodness you have uniformly extended toward me, for your forgiveness of many defects, and your patient and even partial acceptance of every endeavor to serve you; for the liberal provision you have ever made for my maintenance; and for a thousand acts of kindness, which have comforted and assisted me.

To the proprietors, I owe a particular acknowledgment, for their recent generous vote for the continuance of my salary, and hereby ask their leave to relinquish the emolument at the end of the present month. And now, brethren and friends, having returned into your hands the trust you have honored me with — the charge of public and private instruction in this religious society, I pray God, that whatever seed of virtue we have sown and watered together, may bear fruit unto eternal life.

I commend you to the Divine Providence. May He grant you, in your ancient sanctuary, the service of able and faithful teachers. May He multiply to your families and to your persons, every genuine blessing; and whatever discipline may be appointed to you in this world, may the blessed hope of the resurrection, which He has planted in the constitution of the human soul, and confirmed and manifested by Jesus Christ, be made good to you beyond the grave. In this faith and hope, I bid you farewell.

Your affectionate servant,

RALPH WALDO EMERSON.

LETTER OF PROTEST

CONCORD, September 23d, 1846.

DR. S. G. HOWE, AND ASSOCIATES OF THE COMMITTEE OF CITIZENS: — If I could do or say anything useful or equal to the occasion, I would not fail to attend the meeting on Thursday. I feel the irreparable shame of Boston of this abduction. I hope it is not possible that the city will make the act its own, by any color or justification. Our State has suffered many disgraces, of late years, to spoil our pride in it, but never any so flagrant as this, if the people of the Commonwealth can be brought to be accomplices in one crime, — which, I assure myself, will never be. I hope it is not only not to be sustained by the mercantile body, but not even by the smallest portion of that class. If the merchants tolerate this crime, — as nothing will be too bad for their desert, — so it is very certain they will have the ignominy very faithfully put to their lips. The question you now propose, is a good test of the honesty and manliness of our commerce. If it shall turn out, as desponding men say, that our people do not really care whether Boston is a slave-port or not, provided our trade thrives, then we may, at least cease to dread hard time and ruin. It is high time our bad wealth came to an end. I am sure I shall very cheerfully take my share of suffering in the ruin of such a prosperity, and shall very willingly turn to the mountain to chop wood, and seek to find for myself and my children labors compatible with freedom and honor.

With this feeling, I am proportionably grateful

to Mr. Adams and yourselves, for undertaking the office of putting the question to our people, whether they will make this cruelty theirs? and of giving them an opportunity of clearing the population from the stain of this crime, and of securing mankind from the repetition of it, in this quarter forever.

Respectfully and thankfully
Your obedient servant,
RALPH WALDO EMERSON.

LETTER TO WALT WHITMAN

CONCORD, MASSACHUSETTS, 21 July, 1855.

DEAR SIR: — I am not blind to the worth of the wonderful gift of "Leaves of Grass." I find it the most extraordinary piece of wit and wisdom that America has yet contributed. I am very happy in reading it, as great power makes us happy. It meets the demand I am always making of what seemed the sterile and stingy nature, as if too much handiwork, or too much lymph in temperament, were making our western wits fat and mean. I give you joy of your free and brave thought. I have great joy in it. I find incomparable things said incomparably well, as they must be. I find the courage of treatment which so delights us, and which large preception only can inspire.

I greet you at the beginning of a great career, which yet must have had a long foreground somewhere, for such a start. I rubbed my eyes a little, to see if this sunbeam were no illusion; but the solid sense of the book is a sober certainty.

It has the best merits, namely, of fortifying and encouraging.

I did not know until I last night saw the book advertised in a newspaper that I could trust the name as real and available for a post-office. I wish to see my benefactor, and have felt much like striking my tasks and visiting New York to pay you my respects.

RALPH WALDO EMERSON.